KU-646-848

Contents

INTRODUCTION

FACTS ARE ALL around us. Sometimes it seems there are too many facts for our brains to absorb. This book helps your brain by making the facts interesting and easy to understand. The facts are presented in fact panels and data panels on specific subjects, so the facts are easy to find.

Fact Panels

Hundreds of key facts are provided in the fact panels. Each key fact has a bullet (·) to help you find it.

Captions provide additional vital information.

ENCYCLOPEDIA OF
QUESTIONS
AND ANSWERS

ENCYCLOPEDIA OF
QUESTIONS
AND ANSWERS

p

This is a Parragon book
This edition published in 2006

Parragon
Queen Street House
4 Queen Street
Bath BA1 1HE

Copyright © Parragon Books Ltd 1999

This edition put together by Starry Dog Books Ltd

All rights reserved. No part of this publication may be reproduced,
stored in a retrieval system, or transmitted by any means, electronic, mechanical,
photocopying, recording or otherwise, without the prior permission of the copyright holder.

British Library Cataloguing-in-Publication Data

A catalogue record for this book is available from the British Library.

ISBN 1-40545-105-X

Printed in China

Quizzes

At the end of each section is a quiz to test how well you remember the facts. Some of the answers are on the Key Facts pages, so don't forget to read these too!

Categories

The book is broken down into different categories such as animals, science, plants, the Universe etc. to help you find the information you want quickly.

Superb illustrations throughout the book provide visual information to add to your fact-finding.

Amazing Factfinder

This is an atom. It is so tiny that 2 billion would fit on the dot on the top of this 'i'.

This is what a silicon chip looks like from 20cm away. It is about 8mm long.

This is what a butterfly looks like from about 1m away. It is about 2cm across.

This is what a lion looks like from about 10m away. It is about 3m long.

THIS BOOK CONTAINS a huge array of facts about everything from the smallest thing in the Universe to the biggest. The tiniest things in the Universe, like atoms, are so small you can see them only under the most powerful microscopes. The very tiniest are particles called quarks, so small that billions of them would fit inside an atom. The biggest things, like stars and galaxies, are so big you can see them all only when they are very far away. The very biggest is a wall of galaxies in space called the Great Wall, 800 million light years long. In between come all kinds of things, from insects and the little electronic chips that make computers to large animals such as lions and us humans, and from great mountains and rivers to entire continents and the world.

MEASUREMENTS

1,000 picometres	=	1 nanometre
1,000 nanometres	=	1 micrometre
1,000 micrometres	=	1 mm
10 mm	=	1 cm
100 cm	=	1 metre
1,000 m	=	1 kilometre
9,460,000 million km	=	1 light year

SMALL THINGS & BIG THINGS

SMALL THINGS

• A Caesium atom is just 0.0000005 mm across.

• The smallest living thing is the bacterium Mycoplasma laidlawii, 0.1 micrometres long.

BIG THINGS

• The largest galaxy is at the centre of the Abell 2029 galaxy cluster in the constellation of Virgo, thought to be 5.6 million light years across.

• The largest structure made by living things is the coral Great Barrier Reef, off Queensland Australia, over 2,000 km long.

This is what our galaxy the Milky Way looks like from 2 million light years away – that is, about 20 billion billion km. It is about 100,000 light years (about a billion billion km) across.

This is what the Sun looks like from about 140 million km away. It is about 1.3 million km across.

This is what the Earth looks like from 100,000 km away. The Earth is around 13,000km across.

This is what mountains like the Matterhorn in the Alps look like from about 10km away. It is about 3,000m high.

PEOPLE

Heart and blood

THE HEART IS ONE OF THE BODY'S MARVELS, pumping blood around the body ceaselessly. Every second of the day, even as you sleep, the heart's powerful muscles are contracting to send a jet of blood shooting through the body's intricate network of blood vessels. Blood flows right round the body and back to the heart, creating a complete circulation to every part of the body. Without it, you would quickly die. Blood carries the oxygen, nutrients and chemicals that every body cell needs to survive, and washes away all the waste products, including carbon dioxide.

FACTS: About blood

- **What is blood?**
  It is a complex mix of cells and platelets in a clear yellowish fluid called plasma. Washed along in the plasma too are salts, hormones, fats and sugars.

- **Red blood cells**
  The most numerous blood cells are button-shaped 'red' blood cells which are like rafts that ferry oxygen around the body, held on board by a protein called haemoglobin.

- **White blood cells**
  Big 'white' blood cells play a vital role in the body's defence against disease. White blood cells called neutrophils swallow invaders. Lymphocytes help identify them.

- **Platelets**
  Tiny cell fragments called platelets help plug leaks such as cuts.

  ▶ Blood is a mix of red cells (erythrocytes), white cells (leucocytes) and tiny platelets in plasma.

FACTS: About circulation

- **Arteries**
  Blood flows out from the heart through large blood vessels called arteries, which branch into smaller arterioles and then into tiny capillaries.

- **Veins**
  Blood flows back to the heart through small venules that join to form larger veins. The load of oxygen makes blood redder in the arteries than the veins.

- **Double circulation**
  There are two systems of circulation in the body, each pumped by a different half of the heart. The left half of the heart drives the 'systemic' circulation which carries oxygen-rich blood from the lungs around the body. The right half of the heart drives the 'pulmonary' circulation, which drives blood through the lungs to the left side of the heart.

- **Pulse**
  The pumping of the heart sends regular shock waves through the circulation, detectable as a pulse. To feel your pulse, lay two fingers gently on the inside of your wrist. Counting the number of pulses tells you how fast your heart is beating.

DATA: Blood & heart

- **RACING BLOOD**
  Blood flows through the arteries at 1m a second.

- **BLOOD VESSELS**
  There are 60,000km of capillaries in the body.

- **HEART RATE**
  The heart beats on average 80 times a minute.

▲ This doctor is checking his patient's risk of suffering from 'coronary heart disease'. In this disease, the supply of blood to the heart muscle is restricted in some way — and may be cut off altogether, causing a heart attack, in which the heart stops beating.

▶ The heart is not just one pump but two, separated by a thick wall of muscle called the septum. Blood from the veins flows into each half of the heart from the top, flooding the 'atrium', the first of the two chambers. This is a small reservoir where blood builds up before entering the second chamber, or 'ventricle'. The ventricle has extra thick, muscular walls which squeeze the blood out and send it shooting through the arteries.

Blood returning from the body floods from the vena cava into the right atrium

Blood from the left ventricle is pushed into the aorta

Blood goes off to the lungs via the pulmonary artery

Oxygenated blood returns from the lungs

Blood returning from the body gathers in the right atrium

Blood from the right ventricle is pushed into the pulmonary artery

Left atrium

Left ventricle

Valves ensure the blood flows only one way

The body's biggest vein, the inferior vena cava

Septum separating the two halves

The body's widest artery, the aorta

13

Lungs

IF YOU STOPPED BREATHING for more than a minute or two, you would quickly die. Breathing provides your blood with the oxygen from the air that is vital to the survival of every body cell. Just as fire burns only if there is plenty of oxygen, so body cells need oxygen from the blood to break down the food they also get from the blood. Without oxygen, brain cells live only a few minutes – which is why the brain is quickly damaged if the heart stops pumping blood. When cells break down food, oxygen joins with carbon in the food to make carbon dioxide, which you breathe out.

FACTS: About breathing

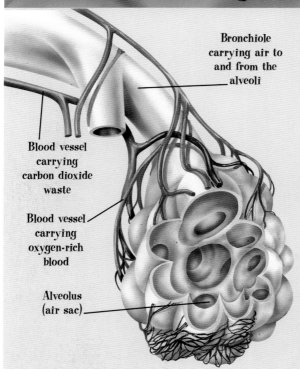

Bronchiole carrying air to and from the alveoli

Blood vessel carrying carbon dioxide waste

Blood vessel carrying oxygen-rich blood

Alveolus (air sac)

▲ At the end of every airway in the lung, there are clusters of tiny air sacs called alveoli — over 300 million altogether. This is where oxygen is transferred into the blood. The 'blue' blood vessels carry carbon dioxide to the alveoli ready for breathing out. The 'red' vessels carry fresh oxygen to the rest of the body.

- **Nose and throat**
  Normally, you breathe air in through your nose — although you can also breathe through your mouth. Air then flows down your throat through a tube — called the pharynx — at the top, the larynx in the middle and the trachea at the bottom.

- **Two lungs**
  The trachea pipes air into your lungs, the two spongy greyish-pink bags in your chest. Lungs transfer oxygen from the air into the blood.

- **Airways**
  The lungs are like hollow trees with hundreds of branching airways called bronchioles.

- **Air sacs**
  Around the end of each bronchiole are clusters of air sacs or 'alveoli', like bunches of grapes.

- **Air to blood**
  When you breathe in, oxygen from the air passes through the thin walls of the alveoli into the tiny blood vessels wrapped around them.

- **Blood to air**
  Unwanted carbon dioxide passes from the blood through the alveoli walls into the lungs — and so goes out of the body as you breathe out.

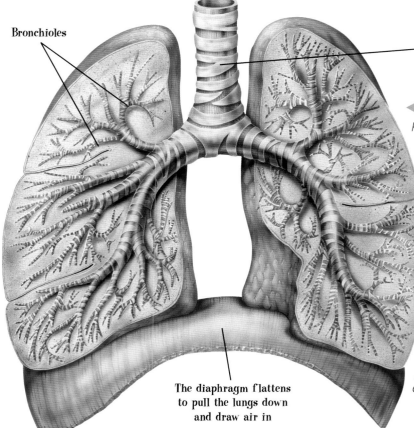

Bronchioles

The trachea or windpipe
funnels air into the lungs

◀ *Your lungs contain miles of airways to provide a huge area for oxygen to seep through into the blood in the short space of each breath. Breathing out requires no effort, because the spongy, elastic material of the lungs just collapses like a balloon when you 'exhale' (breathe out). But to breathe in, muscles in the chest must pull to make the lungs expand. Intercostal muscles between the ribs lift the ribcage (the chest's framework of bone) upwards and outwards. At the same time, a domed sheet of muscle beneath the lung, called the diaphragm, flattens out, pulling the lungs down and further expanding them.*

The diaphragm flattens
to pull the lungs down
and draw air in

DATA: Breathing

- **BREATHS IN A LIFETIME**
  You take about 600 million breaths during your lifetime.

- **LUNG AREA**
  Opened out and laid flat, the lungs would cover an area the size of a tennis court.

- **LUNG CAPACITY**
  On average, we breathe in and out roughly a litre of air every ten seconds or so.

- **LENGTH OF AIRWAYS**
  The branching of the bronchioles means that altogether there are probably over 2,400km of airways in the lungs!

FACTS: Respiration

- **What is respiration?**
  Respiration not only means breathing but also the conversion of sugar to energy in body cells. This conversion is called burning, because it creates heat.

- **Aerobic respiration**
  Aerobic respiration is when muscle cells burn sugar with oxygen. Anaerobic respiration is when they burn sugar without oxygen.

▲ *There is not enough time during a sprint to boost the oxygen supply to the muscles, so they work anaerobically. Only on longer runs do they begin to work aerobically.*

15

Muscles

EVERY MOVE YOU MAKE – running, dancing, smiling and everything else – depends on muscles. You even need muscles to sit still: without them, you would slump like a rag doll. Muscles are bundles of fibres that tense and relax to move different parts of the body, and there are two kinds: muscles that you can control, called voluntary muscles, and muscles that you can't, called involuntary muscles. Most voluntary muscles are 'skeletal muscles', muscles that move parts of your body when you want to. Involuntary muscles are muscles like those of your heart and around your gut, which work automatically.

FACTS: About muscles

▲ The body is covered with an almost complete sheath of skeletal muscle pairs, making up 40 per cent of the body's weight. There are more than 600 all told, the largest of which is the gluteus maximus in the buttock. In theory, you can control each muscle pair individually. But most work in combinations so well-established by habit that they always work together.

• **Muscle pairs**
Muscles work by getting shorter, pulling two points together, then relaxing. So most muscles come in pairs: one to pull, the other to pull it back. Typically, there is a 'flexor' to bend or flex a joint, and an 'extensor' to straighten it again.

• **Muscle fibres**
Muscles are bundles of fibre-like cells. Some contain just a few hundred, others a quarter of a million or more.

• **Striped strands**
Most skeletal muscle fibres are made of thin strands called myofibrils. All along the myofibrils are dark and light stripes called striations which are actually two alternating substances — actin and myosin.

FACTS: About muscles and exercise

• Red muscle and white muscle
Slow-twitch 'red' muscle fibres are good for prolonged gentle movements. 'White' fibres are for short, powerful bursts. Fast-twitch red ones work for both.

◀ *A sportsman trains to develop big muscles, big lungs and a strong heart.*

• Oxygen boost
When muscles work hard they need more oxygen to burn sugar. So when you run your breathing gets faster and deeper, and your heart pumps faster and harder to boost blood supply. A fit person develops bigger lungs and a strong heart. If you're unfit, a long run makes you pant and your heart beat fast.

▼ *In the muscles you use for movement are thousands of long fibres, each made up from hundreds of thinner strands called myofibrils. Alternate bands of actin and myosin filaments in the myofibril give this kind of muscle a stripy or striated look. These filaments interlock and draw together to make the muscle contract.*

▶ *In the upper arm, the biceps at the front is the flexor muscle that contracts (and swells) to bend the arm. The triceps at the back is the extensor that contracts to straighten it out again.*

Muscle made from bundles of muscle fibres

Myofibril made from alternating bands of actin and myosin filament

Muscle fibres are made up from hundreds of myofibrils

Actin filament

Myosin filaments are equipped with hooks like velcro which pull the actin

• How muscles contract
In the muscle fibres, filaments of actin and myosin interlock. When the brain sends the muscle a message to contract, little buds on each myosin filament twist sharply, pulling on actin filaments and contracting.

• Shortening power
There are millions of actin and myosin filaments in each muscle. When they pull together, they can shorten the muscle by almost half its length.

• Smooth muscle
Not all muscles are stripy. Muscles called smooth muscles contract blood vessels to control blood flow to the gut to push food through. The heart is powered by 'cardiac' muscle, which beats automatically, though its rate may vary.

Bones

YOUR BODY IS SUPPORTED by a strong frame called the skeleton. The skeleton not only provides an anchor for muscles, but makes a mount for skin and other tissues, and protects the heart, brain and other organs. It is made of over 200 bones, linked by a rubbery substance called cartilage. Bones are very tough and light because their outside is made from a mixture of hard minerals such as calcium, and stringy, elastic collagen. Inside the tough, dry casing, there are holes called lacunae full of living cells called osteocytes, which are bathed in blood - just like every other cell in the body.

FACTS: About joints

- **Moving joints**
  Joints allow the bones of the skeleton to move. The shoulder is a ball and socket joint. The knee and elbow are hinges, like a door hinge. The neck is a swivelling joint, allowing the head to rotate.

- **Spinal joints**
  The joints between backbones are 'cartilaginous', joined by layers of cartilage which are stiff but allow a little movement.

- **Knee joints**
  Knee joints are lubricated by capsules of oil called synovial fluid, so are called synovial joints.

◀ Skiing and other sporting activities put a tremendous strain on the knee joints, but the joints are protected by a sleeve of tough collagen fibre and lubricated by synovial fluid.

▼ The skeleton is a strong but remarkably mobile framework. It has two main parts. The main or 'axial' part of the skeleton is the skull, spine, ribs and sternum (breastbone). The bones of the 'appendicular' skeleton — arms and legs, along with the shoulders and pelvis (hip-bone) — hang from the axial skeleton.

Cranium (skull)

Scapula (shoulder blade)

Humerus (upper arm)

Rib

Sternum (breastbone)

Radius (main forearm)

Ulna (lesser forearm)

FACTS: About bones

- **Fusing bones**
  Babies have over 300 bones, but many fuse together as they grow, so adults have just 206.

- **Strong bones**
  Weight for weight, bone is five times stronger than steel.

- **Long and short bones**
  The longest, strongest bone is the thigh-bone, or femur. The smallest is the stirrup in the middle ear.

- **Bone make-up**
  Bone is made up from a network of collagen (protein) fibres filled with calcium and phosphate.

- **Bone breakers**
  Fresh bone material is constantly being made in cells called osteoblasts. Old bone is broken down by osteoclasts.

- **Bone marrow**
  In the hollow centre of the breastbone, ribs and hips is soft, spongy red 'marrow' where red and white blood cells are created. All your bones have this red marrow when you are born, but as you grow older, the marrow of long bones such as the legs and arms turns yellow.

▼ *Bones have a surprisingly complex structure. On the outside there is a strong casing of 'compact' bone made of tiny tubes called 'osteons'. Inside this is a layer of spongy bone. Inside this is the marrow.*

Covering membrane or 'periosteum'

Compact bone made of osteons

Spongy bone forms an inner layer

Spongy red marrow makes blood cells, and yellow marrow stores fat

Patella (knee-cap)

Tarsals (ankle-bones)

Phalanges (toe-bones)

Femur (thigh-bone)

Fibula (calf-bone)

Tibia (shin-bone)

Pelvis (hip-bone)

Senses

OUR SENSES TELL US what is going on in the world around us. Even when we are asleep, our senses are picking up sensations, some from inside the body, some from outside, and feeding them to the brain via the nerves, which are like the body's telephone wires. We have five main senses to tell us what is going on in the outside world – sight from our eyes, hearing from our ears, smell from our nose, taste from our tongue and touch from most of our skin. Besides this, there are internal senses, such as pain, and the balance organs in the ear, which tell you whether you are standing upright, or moving fast.

FACTS: About sight

The iris controls the size of the pupil, narrowing it in bright light

Optic nerve

Muscles for turning the eye

Retina

Iris

The cornea focuses the picture

The dark 'pupil' is the window into the eye

Tear duct

The lens keeps the picture sharp

▲ The eyes are two tough little balls filled with a jelly-like substance called vitreous humour. Each eye gives you a slightly different view of the world. The brain combines these different views to give you a complete 3D picture.

• Camera-like eye
Eyes are a bit like video cameras. A lens at the front projects the picture on to the back of the eye, called the retina, where millions of light-sensitive cells detect the picture, and transmit it to the brain via the 'optic' nerve.

• Lens and cornea
The eye's main lens is called the cornea, the clear dome in the middle of the eye. The 'lens' just behind it changes shape to keep the picture sharp.

• Rods and cones
The light-sensitive cells in the retina are called rods and cones. Rods work even in dim light, but cannot distinguish colours. Cones can distinguish colours, but do not work in dim light, which is why we do not see colours well at night.

Bitter

Sour

Sweet   Salty

◀ *Smell relies on a small patch of 'olfactory' nerves inside the top of your nose which react to minute traces of chemicals in the air. Taste is a mixture of sensations, including smell. But your tongue has four different kinds of taste receptors, called taste buds. They react to sweet, salty, bitter or sour tastes in food.*

FACTS: About hearing

▽ *The flap of skin on the outside of your head is only one part of the ear, called the outer ear. It just funnels sound down a canal called the ear canal into your head. The real workings of the ear are inside your head. Here are the bones of the middle ear, and the curly tube of the inner ear.*

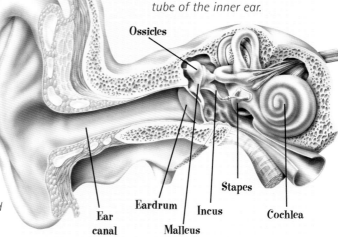

Ossicles

Stapes

Eardrum   Incus   Cochlea

Ear canal   Malleus

▽ *There are touch receptors all over the body, embedded in the skin. They react to four kinds of feeling — a light touch, steady pressure, heat and cold, and pain. Receptors called Meissner's corpuscles are responsible for light touch. Merkel's discs pick up steady pressure.*

Cross-section through the skin

Merkel's disc

Meissner's corpuscle

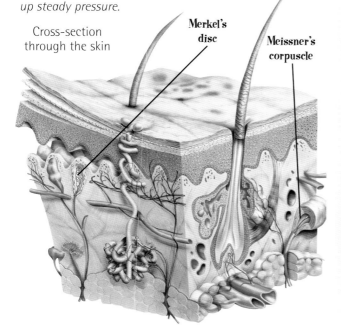

- **The middle ear**
  The middle ear is the ear's amplifier. Sound entering the middle ear hits a taut wall of skin called the eardrum, shaking it rapidly. As it shakes, it rattles three tiny bones or 'ossicles', called the malleus (hammer), the incus (anvil) and the stapes (stirrup).

- **The inner ear**
  The inner ear is mainly a curly tube full of fluid, called the cochlea. As the ossicles rattle, they knock against this tube, making waves in the fluid. Minute detector hairs waggle in these waves and, as they move, they send signals along nerves to the brain.

- **Two ears**
  Because we have two ears, we can detect where a sound is coming from — by the minute differences in loudness between each ear.

The nerves and brain

INSIDE YOUR HEAD IS THE MOST amazingly complex known structure in the universe: the human brain. It looks like a huge, soggy grey walnut with a wrinkled surface. It is split into two halves and weighs on average about 1.5kg. But within this soggy mass are literally billions of intricately interconnected nerve cells. The chemical and electrical impulses continually shooting through your brain cells produce all your thoughts, and control nearly all your actions – and record every sensation – by signals sent to and fro along the remarkable network of nerves that link your body to the brain like the wires in a computer.

FACTS: About the brain

- **Brain damage**
  Brain cells depend on oxygen in the blood. If the supply is cut off for even a few seconds, a person loses consciousness. If it is cut off any longer, cells die and the brain becomes damaged.

- **Parts of the brain**
  The layout of the brain reflects the way it evolved. As it grew out from the primitive brain stem at the top of the spine, it became more complex, developing first into the hind brain, then the complicated cerebrum.

- **The centre of the brain**
  The core of the brain includes the thalamus and brain stem and controls basic functions such as breathing and heart rate, without your awareness. The hypothalamus here controls hunger and sleeping. Around the thalamus is the limbic system which makes you angry or upset.

- **The cerebrum**
  The huge wrinkles of the cerebrum wrap around the core of the brain. This is where you think, and complex tasks such as memory, speech and conscious control of movement go on. All the folds allow a huge number of nerve cells to be squeezed inside the skull.

Cerebrum: thinking, memory, speech, eyesight, hearing and much more

Limbic system: emotion

Thalamus: relay post

Hypothalamus: hunger, thirst and sleeping

Pons

Medulla

Brain stem (medulla and pons): heart rate, breathing

Cerebellum: coordination

Spinal cord

▲ Different areas of the brain are associated with different tasks, such as walking or speaking. Some regions, known as sensory areas, receive signals from sense organs. Others, known as motor areas, are the areas that help you to control muscles and enable you to move.

FACTS: About nerve cells

▼ *Nerve cells receive signals from other nerve cells through tiny branches called dendrites and send them out along a thin, winding tail, or axon. At the far end of the axon the signal is sent on to other cells across tiny gaps called synapses.*

Axon

Synapse

Nucleus

Dendrite

Axon of another nerve cell

- **Nerve cells**
  Nerve cells or 'neurons' are long lived, but when they die, they are not replaced by others.

- **Multi link**
  The nervous system is a network of long strings of nerve cells linked together like beads on a string.

- **Neurotransmitters**
  Nerve signals are sent across synapses, the gaps between nerves, by shots of chemicals called neurotransmitters. Different receptors pick up different neurotransmitters.

◀ *Brain scans show scientists what is going on inside a living brain, and so they now know a great deal about the way the brain works. This has helped them identify, for instance, which areas are active when you are speaking.*

DATA: Nerve facts

- **NERVE SPEED**
  The fastest nerve signals travel at 120m per second.

- **NERVE LENGTH**
  Axons vary from 1mm to 1m long.

- **BRAIN CONNECTIONS**
  There are 100 billion cells in your brain, each connected to as many as 25,000 others.

▶ *The network of nerves in the body — called the nervous system — focuses on the Central Nervous System, or CNS. This includes the brain and the spinal cord (the bundle of nerves in the spine). From the CNS, nerves branch out all over the body.*

New life

LIKE MOST HUMANS, your life probably began when your mother and father made love. Inside your father's body are 'reproductive organs' that are always making millions of tiny cells called sperm, which are like tiny tadpoles. Inside your mother's body are reproductive organs that release an egg into her womb at a certain time every month. Your life began when your mother and father made love at the right time, so that one of your father's sperm worked its way into an egg and fertilized it. The fertilized egg grew gradually inside your mother's womb, until, at last, after nine months or so, you were born.

FACTS: About reproductive organs

- **Puberty**
  You are born with reproductive or sexual organs, but they only develop in the right way for you to have children once you reach the age of puberty — typically 11–13 years. At puberty, chemicals called sex hormones flood through your body, stimulating the changes that turn boys into men and girls into women.

- **Puberty in boys**
  When a boy reaches puberty, his testes grow and begin to produce sperm. At the same time, he begins to grow pubic hair and hair on his chin.

- **Puberty in girls**
  When a girl reaches puberty, she begins to grow breasts, and her monthly periods, or menstruation, start. She, too, grows pubic hair.

- **Menstruation**
  Menstruation is the monthly cycle of changes in a woman's body that prepares her for having a baby. Every four weeks, her ovary releases an egg so that it slides down the Fallopian tube and into her womb. If the egg is not then fertilized, the lining of the womb breaks down and blood flows out of the woman's vagina.

Vas deferens

◀ In a man's reproductive organs, the sperm is made in the two testes or testicles. When making love, the man's erect penis is inserted into a woman's vagina. When the penis is stimulated enough, a liquid called semen carries the sperm from the testes out through the end of the penis into the vagina.

Testicle **Urethra** **Penis**

Fallopian tube

Ovary

Womb, or uterus

Vagina

◀ In a woman's reproductive organs, eggs are stored in the two ovaries. One egg is released a month into the womb, or 'uterus', via the Fallopian tubes. During love-making, millions of sperm from a man's penis enter the woman's vagina and swim up into the uterus, where only one sperm may penetrate an egg.

FACTS: About pregnancy

▲ The moment a sperm enters an egg and fertilizes it is called conception. This is the moment a pregnancy begins. A baby is born about nine months later.

• **Embryo to foetus**
During the first eight weeks of pregnancy, while internal organs are developing, the new life is called an embryo. After that it is called a foetus (say 'feet-us').

• **Life line**
The foetus is supplied with oxygen and food via a tube called the umbilical cord. This links the foetus to the placenta, a spongey organ on the womb lining.

DATA: Ova and embryos

• **FERTILE PERIOD**
An egg or ovum can be fertilized only in the 12–24 hours after it is released (called ovulation).

• **GROWING LIFE**
At four weeks, an embryo is no bigger than a grain of rice, but once it becomes a foetus it grows rapidly. At 20 weeks, a foetus is 25cm long.

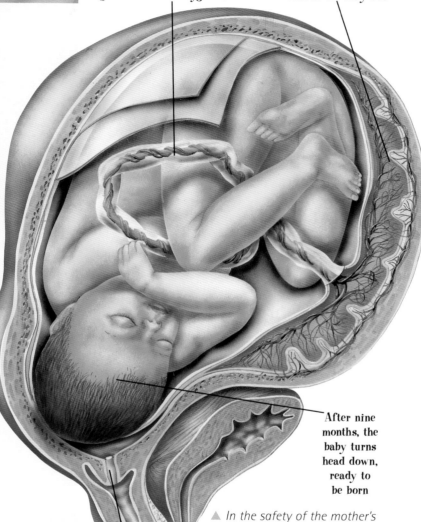

The umbilical cord carries the blood supply from the mother that gives the foetus oxygen and food

The placenta is shed after the birth and follows the baby out

After nine months, the baby turns head down, ready to be born

Cervix, known together with the vagina as the birth canal

▲ In the safety of the mother's womb, the new human life grows from just a few cells to an embryo, then a foetus, to become a baby in nine months, growing larger and more recognizably human by the day. Throughout this time, it is kept warm and cushioned from the outside world inside a bag or sac of fluid called amniotic fluid. When it is ready to be born, the neck of the womb begins to expand, so that the baby can be pushed out through the vagina and into the world.

25

Food and waste

BEFORE YOUR BODY CAN USE any of the food you eat, it must be broken down into simple chemical molecules. This is called digestion. It begins the moment you put food in your mouth and chew it until soft. It continues as you swallow the food and it is pushed down the long tube through your body called the alimentary canal, or gut. A barrage of chemicals and squeezing muscles assault the food all the way through the gut until most is ready to be absorbed through the gut and carried to the rest of the body in the blood. Food that cannot be digested goes out through the anus.

FACTS: About waste disposal

- **Cleaning the blood**
  Toxic chemicals and excess water often build up. It is the task of the kidneys to filter these out of the blood and concentrate them into urine.

- **Kidney**
  The kidneys are two bean-shaped organs in the middle of the back. As they filter blood, they regulate body fluid and salt levels and control blood acidity. They filter seven litres of blood an hour.

- **Ureter and bladder**
  The ureters are the tubes that pipe urine continually from the kidneys to the bladder, a bag where urine builds up until you are able to empty it. The bladder can hold up to half a litre of urine.

- **Urethra**
  When you urinate, urine from the bladder drains out of the body through the urethra. This is 20cm long in men, but just 4cm long in women.

- **Urine**
  Urine is 95% water but contains the poison urea, made in the liver.

  ▶ *The kidneys, ureters, bladder and urethra together make up the urinary system, the body's liquid waste disposal system. Urine is all that is left after valuable ingredients are retrieved by the kidneys from the blood.*

Blood is filtered in bundles called glomeruli

Main vein returning blood to the heart

Kidney

Ureter

Bladder

Urethra

FACTS: About digestion

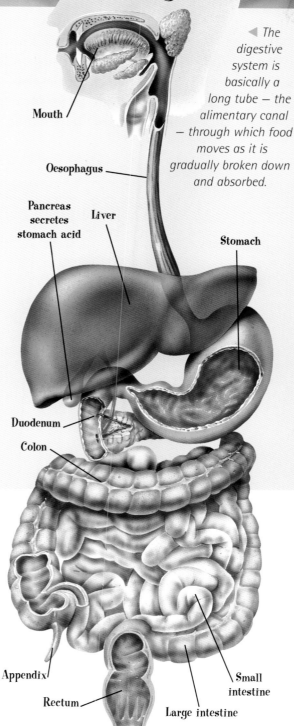

Mouth

Oesophagus

Pancreas secretes stomach acid

Liver

Stomach

Duodenum

Colon

Appendix

Rectum

Small intestine

Large intestine

◀ The digestive system is basically a long tube — the alimentary canal — through which food moves as it is gradually broken down and absorbed.

- **The stomach**
  Food spends about six hours in the stomach. Here it is churned up by the muscles of the stomach wall and attacked by 'gastric' juices, including hydrochloric acid and powerful enzymes, secreted by glands in the stomach wall.

- **Stomach gate**
  Food is held in the stomach by a ring of muscle called the pyloric sphincter until it is partly digested.

- **Food names**
  A lump of swallowed food is called a bolus. Once partly digested by the stomach it is called chyme.

- **Small intestine**
  From the stomach, food goes into the tube called the small intestine, where it is absorbed into the blood. Food undigested here passes into the large intestine, or bowel, where waste is turned solid.

- **Rippling muscles**
  Food is moved through the gut by ripples of the muscles in the gut wall. Muscles extend in front of the bolus or chyme and contract behind it to push it along. This is called peristalsis.

- **Liver**
  The liver has many functions, including turning digested food into blood proteins.

DATA: Digestion

- **LONG GUT**
  Your gut is folded over so many times that it is six times as long as you are tall – up to 10m.

- **FOOD IN THE BODY**
  Food takes on average 24 hours to pass all the way through the alimentary canal.

The healthy body

THE HUMAN BODY IS REMARKABLY GOOD at taking care of itself, and it has a wide range of mechanisms to help it adjust to different circumstances. But to stay healthy, it needs the right food and regular exercise. Most of the food we eat is fuel burned by the body for energy. But the body also needs small quantities of foods such as proteins which are needed to repair cells and build new ones. It also needs minute traces of chemicals that it cannot make for itself: vitamins and minerals. A healthy diet is one that includes all of these foods in just the right proportion and quantity.

FACTS: About diet

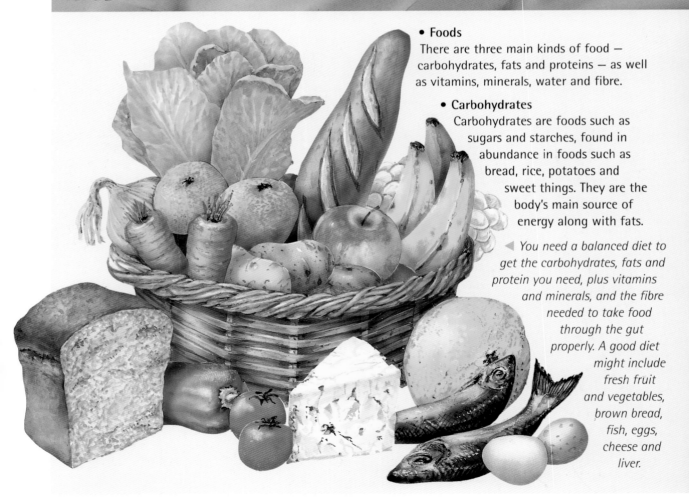

• Foods
There are three main kinds of food — carbohydrates, fats and proteins — as well as vitamins, minerals, water and fibre.

• Carbohydrates
Carbohydrates are foods such as sugars and starches, found in abundance in foods such as bread, rice, potatoes and sweet things. They are the body's main source of energy along with fats.

◄ You need a balanced diet to get the carbohydrates, fats and protein you need, plus vitamins and minerals, and the fibre needed to take food through the gut properly. A good diet might include fresh fruit and vegetables, brown bread, fish, eggs, cheese and liver.

◄ Eating too much carbohydrate-rich and fatty food can cause weight gain. To stay healthy, you should eat these foods in moderate amounts, and exercise regularly to ensure your body is efficient at burning off any excess fat.

- **Fats**
  Fats are greasy foods that won't dissolve in water. Some are solid, such as meat fat and cheese. Others, such as corn oil, are liquid. Fats are not only used by the body as energy stores but are a source of vitamins D and E.

- **Too much fat**
  Too much fat not only makes you fat. Too much 'saturated' fat — mainly animal fat such as butter — can boost the risk of heart disease.

- **Essential acids**
  The body needs 20 'amino acids' to build into protein to make and repair cells. The body can make 12 of these; the other eight it must get from protein in food. These are the 'essential amino acids'.

- **Protein**
  Protein in fish and meat has all the amino acids the body needs. Fruit and vegetables have only some of them, which is why vegetarians must choose the right mixture.

- **Protein sources**
  Beans and nuts are the most protein-rich foods. The protein content in: soya bean flour is 40%; peanuts 28%; cheese 25%; raw meat 23%; raw fish 15%; eggs 12%; bread 8%; rice 6%.

FACTS: Vitamins & minerals

- **Vitamins**
  Vitamins are chemicals vital for life, found in foods. There are 13 major vitamins: A, C, D, E, K and 8 varieties of B. Each has a range of tasks in the body. Vitamin C (in fruit like oranges) helps fight infection and keep gums and teeth healthy. Vitamin A (in foods like carrots, green vegetables and milk) helps keep skin and bones healthy.

- **Essential minerals**
  Essential minerals include small amounts of salt, calcium for bones, iron for red blood cells, and tiny traces of minerals such as iodine.

▲ Vitamins are mostly fairly simple chemicals, such as folic acid (one of the B vitamins), but they are vital for life. This picture shows a vitamin crystal in close-up.

 # DATA: Food

- **FOOD NEEDS**
  On average, people need around 2,000 calories of energy food a day.

- **FOOD INTAKE**
  On average, people in the USA eat 3,200 calories a day. In Ethiopia, they survive on fewer than 500 calories a day.

Sickness and disease

EVERY NOW AND THEN, people succumb to sickness and disease. Most diseases, fortunately, are minor, and the victim usually recovers quickly, thanks to the body's remarkable defence system, called the immune system. Sickness is caused either by an internal failure of one of the body's mechanisms – or by invading microbes or germs. This is where the immune system comes in. The body's immune system not only identifies the germs, but fights them with an array of chemical and biological weapons, including formidable 'immune cells'. Only the very worst diseases defeat the body's immune system.

FACTS: About the immune system

- **The lymphatic system**
  Lymph is a clear fluid that drains from cells into the bloodstream via a network of capillaries, called the lymph system. Immune cells patrol all through the blood, but are concentrated in the lymph system.

- **Inflame response**
  Some germs set off an inflame response. This attacks all germs the same way, increasing blood flow, and bringing a flood of cells called neutrophils into play.

- **Antibodies**
  Antibodies are labels that attach to germs and show killer cells which cells to kill.

- **Killer cells**
  Among the many kinds of immune cells, two kinds of white blood cell are the most important: killer cells, which engulf germs, and B lymphocytes, which identify invaders and make antibodies.

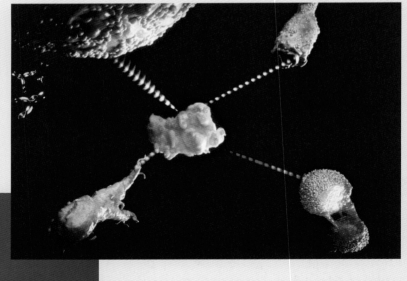

▲ Invaders are targeted by the body's immune system in a number of ways to ensure they are beaten off.

◀ Vaccination is designed to trigger the body to make antibodies against a disease.

FACTS: About germs

◀ *People infected with the HIV virus often succumb to the deadly disease AIDS. This virus is deadly because it attacks the body's immune system and renders it ineffective.*

- **Infection**
  Many germs cause infection, when bacteria, viruses or fungi multiply within your body. As they multiply they either damage cells directly, as viruses do, or may release harmful toxins.

- **Fever and inflammation**
  Infection activates the immune system, and many of the symptoms you feel — fever, weakness, inflammation — are side effects of the immune system's struggle.

- **Bacteria and viruses**
  Viruses are very tiny and can multiply only by entering other cells — such as your body's cells — and taking them over. Bacteria are much bigger, and are tiny one-celled organisms.

DATA: Immune cells

- **ANTIBODY NUMBERS**
  There are thousands of different antibodies in the blood, each targeted against a particular 'antigen' (invader).

- **GIANT EATER**
  A single 'macrophage' (giant eater) T cell can eat up to 100 bacteria.

▼ *Unlike viruses, bacteria can multiply outside the body and can be grown in dishes of protein to create 'cultures'. By growing cultures, scientists can test antibiotic drugs on them and see which are the most effective at killing them off.*

▲ *A common form of allergy is hay fever. In the summer, grasses and other plants release pollen. When this is inhaled, it can cause allergic reactions in some people, like streaming eyes and sneezing.*

What's wrong?

BEFORE YOU CAN BE TREATED for any illness or injury, the doctor has to decide just what is wrong. This is called diagnosis. The most important clues for a diagnosis are usually the symptoms – that is, all the signs that something may be wrong – a cough, a rash, a pain in your side, and so on. The doctor may also find clues in the story of events that led up to the illness, called the history. The illness or injury can often be identified from the symptoms and history alone. If not, you may have to undergo various tests, or have pictures taken of your insides with X-rays or scanners.

FACTS: Looking for clues

- **History**
  Most visits to the doctor begin with the history. While you tell the doctor your symptoms, he or she asks you other questions about the course of events, takes notes and begins to form an idea about the nature of the problem.

- **The examination**
  The doctor may then go on to look at and listen to the appropriate parts of your body where they think there may be further clues. This is called the physical examination. A doctor may look at your eyes using a device called an ophthalmoscope, for instance, or tap on your tummy to hear if the taps vibrate through your internal organs normally. They may also check your temperature or blood pressure.

▼ In the physical examination, the doctor may listen to your chest (right) or check your blood pressure (below).

- **Listening to the chest**
  The doctor can tell a great deal just by listening to your chest using a stethoscope. A stethoscope is a simple listening tube. The tight membrane picks up slight sounds inside your body and the tube transmits them to the doctor's ears. Stethoscopes are particularly important for any problems connected with your breathing or heart.

◄ Athletes continually monitor their bodies – whether they are ill or not – to check that they are achieving peak performance.

FACTS: About CT and other scans

- **CT scans**
  CT or Computerized Tomography scans use computers to build up a series of pictures showing slices through the body.

- **How CT works**
  Inside a CT scanner, an X-ray gun rotates around the patient, firing as it goes. Light detectors on the far side pick up the rays. A computer analyses what happened to each ray as it passed through the patient's body to build up a detailed picture.

- **MRI scans**
  MRI or Magnetic Resonance Imaging uses a powerful magnet to line up all the protons (tiny atomic particles) in a patient's body. A brief pulse of radio waves then knocks them briefly out of alignment. As they snap back into alignment afterwards, they send out little radio signals themselves. The scanner picks up all these billions of tiny signals to give a detailed picture of the body inside.

▼ *CT scans are especially good at showing deep inside the brain, and have revolutionized the treatment of head injuries.*

The X-ray gun rotates round the porthole firing low dose X-ray beams

◄ *For a CT scan, the patient lies on a moving bed and slides into a porthole in the scanner.*

FACTS: About X-rays

- **X-rays**
  X-rays are a simple and effective way of taking a black and white picture of the inside of your body.

  ▶ *This is an X-ray of someone's chest. The ribcage shows up clearly as pale, curved bars.*

- **X-rays**
  X-rays are a bit like light, but they are made from waves too short to see — and they can pass straight through certain tissues in your body to turn photographic film black. Tissues that block their path show up white on film.

Treatments and cures

YOUR BODY HAS ITS OWN RANGE OF defences against illness, called the immune system, and it can fight off many diseases unaided if you are fairly fit. But doctors have many treatments to help when the immune system cannot cope. Some are so effective that many illnesses which were once inevitably fatal, such as tuberculosis, can often now be treated with drugs. Many diseases can be prevented by vaccination programmes, which make the most of the body's immune system. Germs – little organisms such as bacteria and viruses which cause illness – can also be kept at bay by proper hygiene.

FACTS: About drugs

- **Antibiotics**
  Many illnesses that are caused by bacteria can be treated with drugs called antibiotics. These were originally made from moulds and fungi, but are now made synthetically. They include penicillin and tetracycline.

- **How drugs are made**
  In the past, drugs mostly came from natural substances. Now most are made in the laboratory or designed on computer. A few drugs are made by manipulating the genes of living organisms so that they produce the drug. Insulin, for instance, is made in the pancreas of pigs or oxen.

◀ The range of different drugs a doctor has to treat illnesses is now enormous. Most come as pills that can be swallowed, but a few are injected directly into the blood with a needle.

FACTS: About vaccination

▶ This is the germ that causes the terrible disease AIDS, magnified tens of thousands of times. The germ is a virus which attacks the body's immune system. Doctors are looking for a vaccine against it.

▼ Most children have vaccinations at regular intervals as they grow up, against diseases such as diphtheria, whooping cough and tetanus.

▲ Many vaccines are made by genetic engineering — that is, by altering the genes of the germ to make it harmless. These are called live attenuated organisms.

- **Disease protection**
  You can be protected from some diseases by immunization or vaccination.

- **Passive immunization**
  For immediate, short-lived protection from an infection, you might be injected with blood from someone who has already survived the disease. The blood contains tiny proteins called antibodies which defend your body against the invading germ.

- **Active immunization**
  For long-term protection, you may be injected with a killed or mild version of the germ. Your body then makes its own antibodies against the germ, and so is resistant to further infection.

- **Killing diseases**
  Many once common diseases – diphtheria, polio, measles and whooping cough – are now quite rare thanks to mass vaccination of children. Smallpox is now very rare indeed.

▶ The way ordinary hospitals and doctors treat illnesses is based on science and is called conventional medicine. But there are many alternative approaches. Some are based on traditional methods passed down from generation to generation over thousands of years. Many people in Africa go to a witch doctor (right). Other alternatives include herbal medicine which uses herbs as treatments, and Chinese acupuncture, which uses needle pricks in carefully chosen places.

▼ When people are ill, proper care may be as important as the right medicines. If you are only mildly ill, your family or friends can look after you. In hospital, you may be tended by nurses, who make sure you are taking medicines correctly, and provide the right food and fluids.

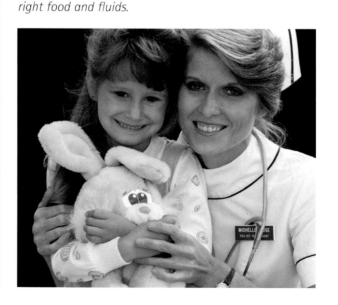

Body repairs

SOMETIMES, WHEN YOUR BODY cannot heal itself, or when treatment with drugs is inappropriate, the only solution may be to cut it open and physically repair it, just as you would a broken-down car. This is called surgery. Surgeons might cut open your body to cut out a diseased or wrongly functioning organ, such as your appendix, or mend a broken bone. They might also, if you are very ill, take out an organ from your body and replace it with a healthy organ from another person (maybe from someone who has died). This is called a transplant.

FACTS: About surgery

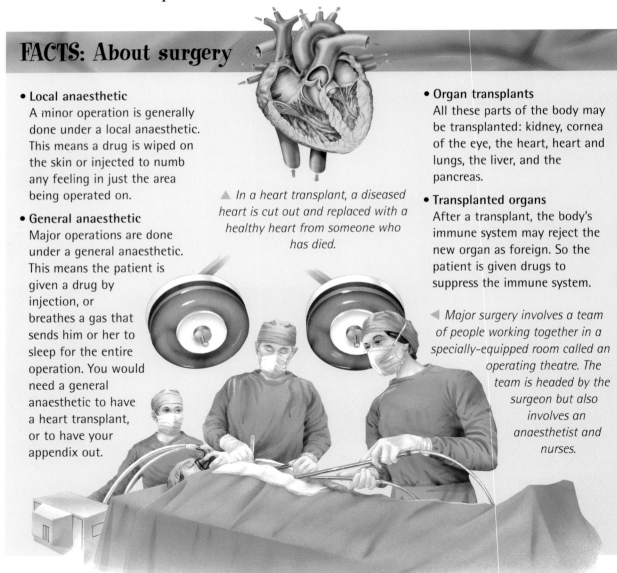

- **Local anaesthetic**
  A minor operation is generally done under a local anaesthetic. This means a drug is wiped on the skin or injected to numb any feeling in just the area being operated on.

- **General anaesthetic**
  Major operations are done under a general anaesthetic. This means the patient is given a drug by injection, or breathes a gas that sends him or her to sleep for the entire operation. You would need a general anaesthetic to have a heart transplant, or to have your appendix out.

▲ In a heart transplant, a diseased heart is cut out and replaced with a healthy heart from someone who has died.

- **Organ transplants**
  All these parts of the body may be transplanted: kidney, cornea of the eye, the heart, heart and lungs, the liver, and the pancreas.

- **Transplanted organs**
  After a transplant, the body's immune system may reject the new organ as foreign. So the patient is given drugs to suppress the immune system.

◀ Major surgery involves a team of people working together in a specially-equipped room called an operating theatre. The team is headed by the surgeon but also involves an anaesthetist and nurses.

FACTS: About implants and prosthetics

- **Implants**
  Sometimes, damaged or diseased parts of the inside of the body such as the hip-bone may be replaced by purpose-made parts made of materials such as metal and nylon. These are called implants.

- **Pacemakers**
  People with heart problems, for instance, may be given a pacemaker, a tiny electronic device that sends out electrical signals to the heart muscles to keep the heart beating steadily.

- **Prosthetics**
  Prosthetics are artificial parts attached to the outside of the body. Someone who has lost an arm, for instance, may be given an artificial one, complete with hinged elbow and movable fingers.

▶ *Implants have to be made of tough, non-corrosive material. This illustration shows parts of the body that may be replaced by implants made of the metal titanium — the same tough, shiny metal that is often used in aircraft.*

▼ *Using a microscope, a microsurgeon can carry out operations on a minute scale — to connect fine blood vessels in the eye, or rejoin minute nerves and tendons severed in an injury.*

Key facts: People

People: tallest, shortest, oldest, youngest

- The tallest man ever was the American Robert Wadlow (b. 1918) who reached a towering 272cm tall.
- The shortest man ever was Gul Mohammed from India (1957–97), who was just 57cm tall when examined in 1990.
- The heaviest man ever was American Jon Minnoch who weighed 635kg when he died in 1983.
- The lightest human adult ever was the Mexican girl Lucia Xarate who weighed just 2.13kg when she was 17 in 1889.

- There is a woman in Africa who is thought to be 150 years old, but no one can prove it.
- In 1997, Frenchwoman Jeanne Calment died aged 122 years and 164 days.
- In 1986, Japanese Shigechiyo Izumi died aged 120 years and 237 days.
- The most children born at once were decaplets — 2 boys and 8 girls born in 1946 in Bacacy in Brazil.
- Mr and Mrs Vassileyev who lived near Moscow in 1782 had 69 of their own children.

Inside the body

- There are over 600 billion cells in your body.
- There are over 200 different types of cell in your body.
- There are 100 billion nerve cells in your brain.
- 14% of your body weight is bone; 40% is muscle.
- You have 213 bones in your body.
- Babies have 300 bones.
- There are 22 bones in your skull.
- There are 33 bones or vertebrae in your spine.

- You have 7 pairs of true ribs, 3 false ribs and 2 floating ribs.
- There are 27 bones in your hand.
- The longest bone is the femur or thigh-bone.
- You have 640 muscles in your body.
- The longest muscle is the sartorius on the inside of the thigh.
- The biggest muscle in your body is the gluteus maximus or buttock.

Breath facts

- You will probably take about 600 million breaths if you live to the age of 75.
- Every minute you are alive, you breathe in more than 6 litres of air.
- A normal breath takes in about 0.4 litres of air. A deep breath can take up to 4 litres.
- On average, you breathe about 13–17 times a minute.
- If you run hard, you may have to breathe up to 80 times a minute.
- Newborn babies breathe about 40 times a minute.
- There are about 300 million little air sacs or alveoli in your body.
- Opened out and laid flat your lungs would cover an area about the size of a tennis court.
- There are over 2,400km of airways in your lungs.

Blood count

- Your heart beats 30 million times each year.
- The chambers of the heart each hold about 70ml of blood.
- Pulse rates average 60 to 100 beats a minute.
- Blood travels through the capillaries at 1m a second.
- There are 60,000km of capillary in your body.
- Capillaries may be just a hundredth of a millimetre thick.
- Someone who weighs 75kg has about 5 litres of blood.
- Someone who weighs 35kg has 2.5 litres of blood.
- Someone who weighs 75kg and lives on the high Andes has about 6 litres of blood.
- A microlitre of blood holds 4-6 million red blood cells.
- A microlitre of blood holds 5-10,000 white blood cells.
- A microlitre of blood holds 150,000–500,000 platelets.
- Blood is 60% plasma.
- Plasma is 90% water.
- There are 13 blood clotting factors, numbers I–XIII.
- There are 4 blood groups: A, O, N and ABO.
- 85% belong to the blood type Rhesus positive. 15% are Rhesus negative.

Milestones

- 1543: Vesalius created his book *De Humani Corporis Fabrica* – which became the basis of modern anatomy.
- 1550: Gabriel Fallopio's close study of the body revealed tiny structures.
- 1590: Santorio Sanctorius created the science of physiology. He also showed how to measure pulse and temperature.
- 1628: William Harvey revealed how the heart circulates blood.
- 1661: Using a microscope, Marcello Malphigi saw tiny blood vessels called capillaries.
- 1798: Edward Jenner showed people could be vaccinated against infectious diseases.
- 1840s: Rudolf Virchow and Jakob Henle found that the body is built up from tissues made from tiny cells.
- 1900: Karl Landsteiner showed that people's blood belongs to different groups.

Key facts: People

Milestones continued

- 1906: Frederick Hopkins suggested the existence of vitamins and that a lack of them caused scurvy and rickets.
- 1920s: Charles Best and Frederick Banting discovered how to control diabetes with insulin.
- 1923: First vaccine for Diphtheria.
- 1927: First vaccine for Tuberculosis.
- 1928: Alexander Fleming accidentally discovered penicillin.
- 1935: First vaccine for Yellow Fever.
- 1940: Howard Florey and Ernst Chain developed penicillin as a working antibiotic.
- 1951: The heart-lung machine was invented.
- 1963: An oral vaccine against polio became available for use.
- 1967: Christiaan Barnard performed the first human heart transplant.
- 1978: Birth of Louise Brown, the first 'test-tube' baby.
- 1980: Smallpox was eradicated worldwide.
- 2003: The Human Genome Project was completed. All the genes in human DNA were identified.
- 2005: The World Health Organization warned of a possible flu pandemic resulting from bird flu mutations.

Record feats

- The longest period of hiccoughing, by American Charles Osborne, lasted for 68 years (1922–90).
- The world's biggest feet belong to American Matthew McGrory. His feet are size 29 UK shoes (European size 63, US size 29.5).
- The longest extension of a human neck is 40cm by the Padaung women of Myanmar.

- The longest interval between the birth of two children to the same mother is 41 years 185 days. Elizabeth Ann Buttle's first child was born in 1956, and the last in 1997, when she was aged 60.
- The shortest interval between two children born in separate confinements is 208 days, by Jayne Bleackley. She gave birth to her son on September 3, 1999, and to her daughter on March 30, 2000.
- The oldest human footprints discovered date back 117,000 years. They were found in South Africa.
- The longest fit of sneezing lasted 978 days, by 12-year-old English girl Donna Griffiths.
- The most blood donated was 188.9 litres (41.5gal) by Maurice Creswick of South Africa.

Body's ingredients

B	C	N	O	F
boron	carbon	nitrogen	oxygen	fluorine
5	6	7	8	9

Si	P	S	Cl
silicon	phosphorus	sulphur	chlorine
14	15	16	17

As	Se	Br
arsenic	selenium	bromine
33	34	35

Te	I
tellurium	iodine
52	53

At
astatine
85

Chemical element	Proportion of total weight (%)	Grams in average adult body
Oxygen	65	39,000
Carbon	18.5	11,100
Hydrogen	9.5	5,700
Nitrogen	3.2	1,920
Calcium	1.5	900
Phosphorus	1	600
Potassium	0.4	240
Sulphur	0.3	180
Chlorine	0.2	120
Sodium	0.2	120
Magnesium	0.1	60

Other main elements: iodine, iron, cobalt, copper, fluorine, manganese, zinc, silicon

Classification - humans

Kingdom:	Animals
Phylum:	Chordates
Subphylum:	Vertebrates
Class:	Mammals
Order:	Primates - lemurs, bushbabies, monkeys and apes
Family:	Hominids - humans and their close relatives
Genus:	Homo 'human'
Species:	Homo sapiens 'wise human'. All human beings are in this group.

Brain facts

• The brain has three main parts:
1) the cerebrum is where thinking and memory take place.
2) the cerebellum coordinates muscular activity such as walking.
   3) the brain stem controls involuntary activity such as breathing.

• Each half (or hemisphere) of the brain works slightly differently:

Left brain
• right-handed skills
• speech
• language, reading and writing
• mental arithmetic
• logic and reasoning

Right brain
• left-handed skills
• creating music
• sculpture, arts, spatial awareness (patterns and shapes)
• imagination and ideas
• visual imagery

41

Quiz: People

1. Vitamin C helps your body fight infection. Which foods are particularly rich in vitamin C?

2. On average, how many calories of energy from food do people need every day?

3. How much air do we breathe in and out every 10 seconds?

4. Blood carries food as well as oxygen to the body cells: true or false?

5. Your pulse – the rate your heart beats – is normally 300 beats a minute: true or false?

6. What are the major blood vessels that carry blood out (away) from the heart called?

7. The tiniest blood vessels are called capillaries: true or false?

8. Your biggest muscle is in your buttocks: true or false?

9. How many muscles do you have in your body - 640 or 1,170?

10. What are the muscles at the front of the upper arm called?

11. Which is the longest bone in your body?

12. What is the spongy red substance called in the hollow centre of the breastbone, ribs and hips?

13. What is the coloured part of your eye called?

14. The back part of the eye, where the image is projected, is called the retina: true or false?

15. The curly tube in your inner ear is called the cockle: true or false?

16. The taste buds on your tongue can detect four different kinds of tastes: salty, bitter, sour and one other - what is it?

17. The brain is the only part of the body that can survive without oxygen: true or false?

18. When nerve cells die, they are not replaced by others: true or false?

19. The tallest man who ever lived was 272cm tall: true or false?

20. What is the name of the tiny electronic device fitted inside people with heart problems?

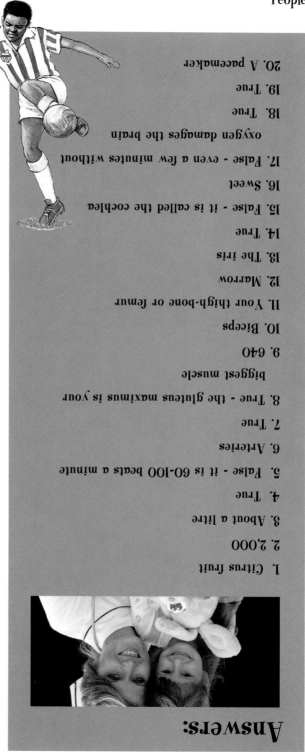

Answers:

1. Citrus fruit
2. 2,000
3. About a litre
4. True
5. False - it is 60-100 beats a minute
6. Arteries
7. True
8. True - the gluteus maximus is your biggest muscle
9. 640
10. Biceps
11. Your thigh-bone or femur
12. Marrow
13. The iris
14. True
15. False - it is called the cochlea
16. Sweet
17. False - even a few minutes without oxygen damages the brain
18. True
19. True
20. A pacemaker

ANIMALS

Small mammals

MAMMALS COME IN ALL SHAPES AND SIZES and live in a huge variety of places, from the frozen arctic wastes to the hottest desert. Like fish, birds, amphibians and reptiles, they are 'vertebrates' – animals with backbones. This really means they have a bony skeleton inside their bodies, which makes a strong frame for hanging everything on. Besides a backbone, mammals usually have two pairs of limbs, a skull to hold the brain, eyes, ears and a nose – and then a heart, lungs and guts inside the ribs.

FACTS: About mammals

- **Warm-blooded**
  Mammals are said to be endothermic (warm-blooded) and reptiles exothermic (cold-blooded). This doesn't mean reptiles' blood is necessarily colder. It just means that mammals are able to keep their blood and bodies equally warm all the time — which is why they can survive in so many different places.

- **Babies**
  All mammals begin life as a tiny egg inside their mother's body. But most young mammals develop inside their mother's body until they are born as babies. Very few baby mammals can cope by themselves when they are born, and most need looking after by their parents for a while. Human babies need looking after for many years.

- **Mammals that lay eggs**
  A few mammals living in Australia called monotremes lay eggs rather than have babies. These include the duck-billed platypus.

The badger is one of 4,200 known species of mammal around the world.

- **Milk-power**
  Unlike other animals, mother mammals feed their babies on milk until they are old enough to cope with solid foods. Milk gives all the fat and protein the baby needs to grow.

- **Milk on tap**
  The more babies a mother mammal tends to have, the more pairs of teats she has. Humans have just one pair, but pigs have seven pairs.

- **Big and small**
  The biggest mammal is the blue whale, 30m long and weighing 150,000kg; the smallest land mammal is the Etruscan shrew, just a few cms long and weighing only 1.5gms.

- **Fur coats**
  All mammals have a fur coat, even if it is just made up of a few strands like with humans, rhinos and whales. Fur keeps the animal warm by trapping a layer of insulating air. Seals have special, oily water-repelling fur and a layer of thick fat called blubber to keep them warm in polar oceans

- **Clever creatures**
  Compared to other animals, much more of a mammal's brain is cerebrum, the part of the brain devoted to intelligent behaviour. In humans and apes, the proportion is biggest of all.

FACTS: About rodents

- **Rodents**
  There are over 1,700 species of rodent, including rats and mice, rabbits and guinea pigs.

- **Front teeth**
  All rodents have two pairs of ever-growing, razor-sharp front teeth, or incisors, for gnawing.

▲ *Weasels are among the most effective of all small predators — they are both agile and strong.*

◄ *Squirrels have fur-lined cheek pouches which they use for storing food.*

▲ *Porcupines are small mammals covered in incredibly long spines which protect them from predators. When threatened, they rustle or rattle their spines — or even run backwards into the enemy, spines pointing.*

▶ *Beavers are the biggest of all rodents, but for the South American capybara. They live in water and use their sharp teeth to gnaw through trees to get wood to dam streams. They build their homes, called lodges, in the pond created behind this dam.*

The inside of the beaver's lodge is above water level, but it is reached by an underwater entrance

Beavers have two very sharp teeth for gnawing

Beavers' big flat tails and webbed back feet make them good swimmers

Large mammals

SOME MAMMALS ARE TINY but the big mammals are the biggest living things in the world. The biggest of all the mammals on land are elephants which can grow up to 4m tall – as high as a double-decker bus – and weigh 7,000kg, which is as much as a big truck. Not that much smaller are two other creatures of tropical Africa and Asia, the rhinoceros and hippopotamus. All of these big mammals are herbivores, which means they eat plants. So, too, are the many medium-sized herd animals like buffalos and horses.

FACTS: About elephants

- **Long nose**
  An elephant's most remarkable feature is its long trunk, or 'proboscis', which it uses for breathing, smelling, pulling down branches, picking up objects, making trumpeting noises and for sucking up water.

- **Long life**
  Elephants live longer than all mammals apart from man, surviving up until the age of 80 in captivity.

- **Big ears**
  When an elephant holds its ears back flat, it is either relaxed, or feeling cowed by another. A dominant or aggressive bull (male elephant) often sticks its ears out.

- **Big teeth**
  Elephants have two giant teeth called tusks which they use for digging or to fend off enemies. Bulls sometimes lock tusks and wrestle with their trunks to see who's strongest.

- **Keeping cool**
  To cool off in the heat elephants stretch out or flap their ears. They also cover themselves with mud or spray themselves with dust or water. Coating their skin like this also helps to condition their skin and provide a protective layer.

- **Herds**
  Elephants live in herds, ranging from four to 30 members, led by a mature cow, or 'matriarch'. The rest of a herd is generally made up of several females and their young, as well as a few young bulls. Adult males tend to move off and live on their own or in all male groups.

Tusks curve as they grow

▶ *Elephants in Africa are much bigger than those found in Asia, with an African bull measuring up to 4m tall and weighing 7,000kg.*

Rhinos such as this Indian rhinoceros have thick, hairless skin which is arranged like protective armour, folding at the neck, shoulders and legs to allow movement. Some species of rhino also have one horn; some have two. These horns are actually made of densely compacted hair, or 'keratin'.

The African elephant has much bigger ears than an Indian elephant, and a sloping forehead instead of a domed one.

Horses belong to a group of mammals called ungulates, or hooved mammals. As with pigs, cattle and camels, claws have been replaced with hooves. Each foot of a horse has one toe with a toenail, which is the hoof. They are very fast runners, using just the tip of this toe as they move.

FACTS: About herbivores

- **Grazers and browsers**
  Herbivores that eat grasses are called 'grazers', while those that eat leaves, bark and the buds of trees and bushes are called 'browsers'. Some animals eat only one kind of plant, but most will actually eat a variety depending on whatever is available.

- **Steady eating**
  Because plants are not as nutritious as meat, most herbivores need to spend large amounts of time eating – unlike carnivores, which feed only occasionally. An elephant, for example, usually feeds for at least 18 hours every day.

The takin (right) is a herbivore that lives in Central Asia. It looks a bit like a goat, but with shorter horns and a stockier body, covered in dense brown hair.

DATA: Large mammals

- **THE BIGGEST ANIMALS**
  Rhinos and hippos are the second heaviest land mammals after elephants. An African white rhinoceros weighs up to 9 tonnes.

- **AN ELEPHANT'S DIET**
  Elephants eat up to 150kg of food per day. They also drink about 180 litres of water a day.

- **HORSE BREEDS**
  There are 150 different breeds of domestic horse.

Big cats

LIONS, TIGERS, JAGUARS, PUMAS AND LEOPARDS are kinds of big cats, found all over the world except Australasia. Although they have the same basic body structure as pet cats, they are very different in other ways. They vary in size considerably, from the big tiger to the tiny wild cat, but big cats are usually much bigger and stronger than pet cats, and they roar and grunt rather than mew and purr. All are deadly hunters, slinking up on their prey then pouncing on it. Their sharp claws, powerful jaws and fangs inflict terrible wounds on victims.

FACTS: About tigers

- **Very big cat**
  Tigers are the largest of the big cats, with huge heads and growing 2.5m long. The long tail adds almost another metre.

- **Disguising stripes**
  Tigers are instantly recognizable by their stripes. But in the forest areas of southern Asia where they live, their black stripes on a gold background act as camouflage. Their chins and stomachs are snowy white.

- **Head hunter**
  Tigers prey on large animals such as deer, buffalo, antelopes and wild pigs, hunting mainly at night. But it takes a tiger a lot of effort to make a kill; nine out of ten times, the victim will actually make a getaway.

- **Endangered tigers**
  Hunters killing tigers for their skins, and farmers clearing the forest for land, have decimated tiger numbers, and they are now restricted to special reserves in Asia, mainly in India and Sumatra.

  ▷ *Tigers are solitary creatures, living alone most of their lives. To keep other tigers out of their territory, they leave urine samples and scratch marks on trees.*

- **Lone males**
  Tigers have their own ranges but a male's may include that of some females. They meet only to mate.

- **Young tigers**
  Two to four tiger cubs are born at a time and live with their mother for 3 years as they learn to survive.

FACTS: About lions

◀ *A male can be up to around 3m long from his nose to the tip of his tail. Males also have a mane, which gets darker as they get older. Females have no mane and are also a bit smaller.*

- **King of the beasts**
  Lions are majestic big cats once found all over southern Asia but now found mainly on the grasslands of Africa. They are the only truly social cats, living together in groups called prides. The adult male lion is instantly recognizable by the big mane that covers its head.

- **What lions eat**
  Lions feed on wildebeest, zebras and antelopes — occasionally giraffes. They have big side teeth and short, strong jaws for eating flesh.

- **Lions on the hunt**
  It is usually the female that hunts, alone or in pairs, although the males are the first to eat once the prey has been caught. The hunting lionesses stealthily approach a victim then make a short dash and pounce on it quickly. If they don't succeed in their short dash, they give up and wait for another opportunity. Only one in four hunts leads to a kill.

- **A quiet life**
  A lion spends 18 hours a day sleeping, since the meat it eats is so nutritious. It eats one solid meal then goes without food for the next few days.

▶ *Among the many smaller big cats is the margay, which lives in the forests of South and Central America and preys on small mammals and birds. The margay is solitary, has good reflexes, keen eyesight and is an excellent climber. However, it has been hunted for its coat and as a result is now quite rare.*

▶ *With its spotted coat, the jaguar is one of the most beautiful of the big cats. It lives in South American forests, usually near water, and hunts peccaries, capybaras and fish. It looks a bit like the leopard of Africa and Asia, but these have black blotches or rings, whereas jaguars have spots with rings around them.*

Monkeys and apes

HUMANS, APES, MONKEYS AND LEMURS all belong to a group of animals called primates. Most of them, except humans, live in places where there are trees, and have hands with fingers, and feet with toes for gripping branches. The apes are our closest relatives in the animal world and have similar long arms, and fingers and toes for gripping. Monkeys have long arms too, but they are usually much smaller, and have a tail for helping them to balance as they swing through the trees. They live all over the world in warm regions.

FACTS: About lemurs and langurs

- **What are lemurs?**
Lemurs are nocturnal animals with big, staring eyes. They have soft, thick fur and bushy tails which they use to intimidate other animals, signal to other lemurs and wave scent around (from glands in their bottoms!).

- **Where lemurs live**
Nearly all lemurs live in forests on the island of Madagascar off the east coast of Africa. They tend to live mostly in trees.

- **Kinds of lemur**
There are 21 species of lemur. Some are brightly coloured, such as the ring-tailed lemur, which has black and white rings all the way down its tail.

- **Tiny primates**
Lemurs are all quite small — the biggest is only as big as a large house cat, while the smallest, the lesser mouse lemur, grows to only 13cm.

- **Langurs**
Langurs are small monkeys that live in the forests of southeast Asia and mainly eat leaves.

▷ *Like other langurs, the Hanuman langur has a strong stomach that can cope with the toughest leaves.*

◁ *Monkeys are divided into those of the Old World and the New World. Old World monkeys, such as the baboon (left), live in the warmer parts of Africa and Asia. They tend to be larger than New World monkeys but do not have prehensile tails (tails that grip). Their backsides are usually naked and their nostrils are close together.*

◁ *New World monkeys live in Central and South American forests. Many, such as the spider monkey (left), have prehensile tails to help them climb and to hang from branches, keeping their legs and arms free for holding food. Their noses are also much wider than those of Old World monkeys and their nostrils face outwards.*

FACTS: About apes

- **Fellow apes**
  Apes are so closely related to humans that some zoologists divide apes into three kinds — lesser apes (gibbons and siamangs), great apes (orang-utans, gorillas and chimpanzees) and man. None has a tail.

- **Great apes and lesser apes**
  Great apes are almost human-shaped, though they tend to have longer arms, big, protruding jaws — and, of course, are covered in fur. They are often very clever, too, especially chimpanzees. Lesser apes are smaller and less clever, but they can be very agile climbers indeed.

- **Chimpanzees**
  Chimps are man's closest relative and the cleverest of the apes. They communicate with varied vocal sounds, gestures and facial expressions. They also use tools such as sticks to get food.

- **Gibbons**
  Gibbons are agile apes which live in southeast Asian forests and swing swiftly from branch to branch — up to 3m in a single swing.

- **Orang-utan**
  Orang-utan is Malay for 'old man of the forest'. They live in the rainforests of Borneo and Sumatra and look like hairy old men.

Gorillas are the biggest of the apes. A big male can be 1.7m tall. They look ferocious, but are among the gentlest of creatures. They eat only berries and leaves, and the male only becomes aggressive when a rival male intrudes on his group — even then he only beats his chest and roars.

Adult males are called silverbacks because they have grey hairs on their backs

The gentle gorilla roars like this only when his family is threatened

53

Pandas, bears & dogs

ALL BIG CARNIVOROUS (MEAT-EATING) ANIMALS are essentially either cats or dogs. Cats are very obviously cats, but the dogs include bears as well as the more obviously dog-like creatures such as wolves, foxes, jackals and coyotes. To a zoologist, a bear is rather like a big dog without a tail. Both bears and dogs are mostly hunters that eat meat, but, unlike cats, bears especially will also eat other things if food is scarce. Surprisingly, although pandas look like bears, they are actually more closely related to raccoons.

FACTS: About wolves, foxes and jackals

- **Big dogs**
  The dog family is a group of 35 species including wolves, foxes, wild dogs, domestic dogs, jackals and coyotes. All dogs have long legs, long narrow muzzles and pointy canine teeth for eating flesh. They all also have a very good sense of smell.

- **Wolf packs**
  To hunt animals bigger than themselves such as moose, deer, caribou or musk oxen, wolves hunt together in packs. Wolf packs use smell to trace their prey, then try to isolate a weak animal within the herd and run it down.

- **Top dog**
  The eldest male and female in a pack maintain a strict hierarchy. Any wolf that tries to challenge their dominance is subdued or even expelled from the pack altogether. A pack may consist of 7-20 wolves.

The red fox is very adaptable and is often found living in cities, surviving by raiding rubbish dumps.

- **Fox**
  Foxes are clever hunters that prowl at night, alone or in pairs. They catch and eat rats, mice and rabbits, but they will also willingly eat whatever is available, such as fruit, birds and even human food scraps.

- **Jackal**
  Jackals live in Africa and Asia and look like small wolves. They hunt alone, not in packs, killing rats, mice and birds. They meet up only when there is a chance of getting in on the leftovers from the kill of a lion or a leopard — their deadliest enemy.

Wolves once lived all over Europe and North America, but they have now been all but exterminated in Europe and live only in remote areas of North America.

FACTS: About bears

- **Where bears live**
  Bears live mostly in the northern hemisphere, in all kinds of environments. Only the spectacled bear lives in South America.

- **Brown bears**
  Brown bears are called 'grizzly' because of the white fur on their shoulders.

- **Polar bears**
  White polar bears live in the Arctic and are the only bears that live on meat alone.

△ Brown bears such as this Himalayan bear hibernate. They put on weight during the autumn and then retreat to a den for winter.

▽ *The giant panda is one of the rarest animals, living only in the mountainous forests of central China where its food, a certain kind of bamboo, grows. The bamboo is not very nutritious, so pandas spend 10–12 hours a day eating. They rarely have cubs, so the birth of a panda is precious.*

Pandas have a pad on their forepaws, called a sixth finger, to help them grip bamboo shoots as they chew

DATA: Pandas, bears and dogs

- **THE BIGGEST BEAR**
  The largest bear is the Kodiak, a type of brown bear from Alaska, which measures up to 2.5m and weighs up to 780kg.

- **THE LITTLEST BEAR**
  The smallest of the bears is the sun bear of the southeast Asian rainforests. It is only about 1.4m tall and 27kg in weight.

- **WOLF RANGE**
  One wolf pack may inhabit a huge territory – up to 1,000 square kms. They also cover great distances when hunting for food.

- **PANDA FOOD**
  Because bamboo has such a low nutritional value, pandas may eat up to 15kg of stems and leaves in a single day.

Sea mammals

MAMMALS ARE WARM-BLOODED CREATURES that breathe air and rear their young on milk. Most are land animals, but they are remarkably adaptable and a few kinds spend all their lives in the sea, swimming around with the ease of a fish and coming up for air only occasionally. There are two main kinds of sea mammal. There are seals, sea lions, walruses and sea cows, which mostly live in cold places and have both fur and a thick layer of fat called blubber to keep them warm. Then there are whales, dolphins and porpoises, which have no fur, only blubber.

FACTS: About whales, dolphins and porpoises

- **Cetaceans**
  Whales, dolphins and porpoises are together known as cetaceans. Many are very gentle and intelligent creatures.

- **Breathing**
  Whales can stay hours under water, but must eventually come up for air and spout out water from a blow hole on top.

Playful leaps, somersaults and spins help knit groups of dolphins together

- **Schools**
  Dolphins live in groups called schools up to 300 strong.

- **Dolphin talk**
  Dolphins keep in touch by clicks, barks, chattering sounds, screams and moans, each of which seem to have a meaning which scientists do not understand. They find their way with sounds too high for the human ear to hear.

- **Whale sound**
  Whales use booming sounds to keep in touch. Finback whales can hear each other 850km apart.

▲ Dolphins are very friendly, playful and intelligent creatures. They form strong social relationships, with close mother-child bonds. Mating pairs seem to stay together for life.

- **Toothed and toothless whales**
  Some whales, such as the sperm and killer whales, have teeth and eat large fish. Others, like the humpback and blue whales have no teeth. Instead, they have special comb-like sieves in their mouths called baleens. They feed by straining tiny, prawn-like creatures called krill through the baleen.

FACTS: About seals, sea lions and walruses

- **Going ashore**
  Seals, sea lions and walruses are agile swimmers, but, unlike whales and dolphins, they can live on land — although once ashore, they tend to waddle.

- **Breeding grounds**
  In spring and summer, thousands of seals crowd together on the shore to breed in vast colonies.

- **Seals and sea lions**
  Seals and sea lions look similar but, while seals have only ear openings, sea lions have ear flaps like most land mammals. Sea lions can also move their back flippers under their body to help them move around on land, unlike seals.

- **Seal meals**
  Seals and sea lions feed mainly on fish, but also eat shellfish. Crabeater seals feed mainly on krill, while bearded seals eat mainly clams.

- **Walruses**
  Walruses are big creatures a little like overgrown seals, growing up to 3m long, but they have massive tusks and face whiskers.

- **Leopard**
  The most ferocious seal is the Antarctic leopard which grows to 4m and feeds on penguins.

▼ *Seals spend most of their lives in the sea, but come ashore to give birth. They stay on land for several weeks in colonies called rookeries, feeding their young milk. Every now and then, hunters will cull (kill) the young pups while they are still ashore — both for their fur and to keep down numbers. Many believe this is cruel. Others say it is necessary.*

▶ *Sea-cows — dugongs and manatees — are plant-eating seals that live in warm coastal waters. Dugongs live around Africa and Asia. Manatees live in coastal rivers in the southeast USA, the West Indies and northern South America. They greet one another with muzzle to muzzle kisses.*

Manatee

57

Pets

PEOPLE HAVE KEPT ANIMALS for many thousands of years – sometimes to help with particular tasks, sometimes as companions, sometimes simply to look at and admire. Dogs were first tamed over 12,000 years ago to help with hunting, and since then many other animals have been adopted as pets – cats, birds, hamsters, guinea pigs, horses and many others. There are more pet owners now than ever before, with millions of animals living in people's homes around the world. There are 500 million cats alone.

FACTS: About cats

- **Egyptian cats**
  The Ancient Egyptians tamed wild African bushcats to catch mice 3,500 years ago. Later, the Egyptians thought cats sacred.

- **Rough tongues**
  Cats' tongues are covered in bristles which help them to lap up liquids and foods and to groom themselves, as with a comb.

- **Catnaps**
  Cats spend a lot of time sleeping — in short naps. But they can be awake and ready for action in an instant.

- **Cat litter**
  Most female cats are ready to be mothers by 10 months old – though many are neutered by their owners to stop them breeding. Female cats are pregnant for 9 weeks and give birth to a litter of 2-5 kittens.

◀ There are many different breeds of cat, from common tabbies and tortoiseshells to valuable pedigree Siamese and Persian cats.

Dogs

There are over 130 different breeds of domestic dog, but all are descended from the wolf, and, even though tame, they retain many wolf-like traits — body language, guarding territory, hiding bones and so on.

▲ Many pets were originally working dogs, like the collie. Originally from Scotland, collies make wonderful sheepdogs. They are fast runners, quick learners and have an amazing sense of smell. They can even locate a sheep lost in the snow.

▶ Some pets were originally hunting dogs, like terriers. Great diggers, with strong teeth and jaws, terriers were once used to dig out rats, rabbits and badgers from the ground, and their name comes from the Latin terra, for earth.

▲ *Hamsters live only for two or three years. Golden hamsters (above) — the small variety kept as pets — all descend from a single wild litter found in Syria in 1930.*

▲ *Many pet dogs come from hunters and gun dogs, such as setters, pointers and retrievers. When a red setter (above) spots a game bird, it crouches slightly and freezes, pointing its nose to the bird for the hunter.*

▼ *St Bernards are one of many dogs used to help in emergencies and were once trained at the monastery of the Great St Bernard Pass in Switzerland to rescue people who got lost in the surrounding mountains.*

FACTS: About fish

- **Tropical fish**
  Small tropical fish such as butterfly fish, angel fish and guppies are kept for their bright colours. But they are used to warm water, so must be kept in heated tanks.

- **Deadly fish**
  Some people like to keep piranhas from the Amazon. They have sharp teeth and are voracious flesh eaters, able to attack in a mass and eat large animals .

▶ *Descended from dull coloured carp, goldfish were carefully bred by the Chinese and Japanese and are now the most popular of all pet fish.*

DATA: Pets

- **BIGGEST DOG**
  The tallest dog of all is the Irish wolfhound – 110cm to the shoulder.

- **HEAVIEST DOG**
  The heaviest dog is the St Bernard – 90kg.

- **SMALLEST DOG**
  The smallest dog is the Chihuahua – 13.8cm tall.

- **OLD CAT**
  Cats may live up to the age of 20.

- **TINY FISH**
  The smallest fish are dwarf gobies, which can be as little as 9mm long.

Farm animals

BACON, HAMBURGERS, SHOES, BUTTER, woollen jumpers, milk and many other things are provided by animals kept on farms – including cattle, sheep, pigs and hens. All these animals are descended from wild animals, but they were domesticated – made tame – many thousands of years ago to give us a steady supply of meat, milk, eggs, fur, wool and leather. Since then, farmers have created many hundreds of breeds of each animal, such as Herefordshire cows and Merino sheep to create a more meaty animal, or one that gives better milk or wool.

FACTS: About cows

- **What are cows?**
  Cows or cattle are descended from the wild auroch tamed 9,000 years ago. Male cattle are bulls; female, cows; and young cattle, calves.

- **Dairy cow**
  Females are reared for milk, butter and cheese and called dairy cows. They give birth to a calf each year and after the birth provide milk twice a day for 10 months.

- **Beef breeds**
  Male cattle are reared for meat. Cattle also provide leather and glue and droppings for fertilizer. Beef breeds are rounder and heftier than dairy cows.

- **Chewing the cud**
  Cows chew the cud. They have four stomachs and after swallowing food they bring it back up into their mouths for further chewing.

▲ Goats are kept for meat, milk, skins and wool. Goats' milk is very good for people who are allergic to richer cows' milk, while Angora and Kashmir goats provide very fine wool. Goats are often kept in rocky mountain areas because they are agile and have strong enough jaws and stomachs to live off coarse vegetation.

▼ Pigs are kept for meat – pork, bacon and ham – and leather. Their hairs are also used to make artists' brushes. The European domestic pig is descended from the European wild boar, which is much hairier and darker than the domestic pig, and also has tusks. Most pigs are now raised on factory farms where they are fed on special diets that help them grow rapidly.

FACTS: About poultry

◁ On a few farms, hens may scratch around for insects and seeds in the farmyard and lay their eggs in a small hut called a coop. These are called free-range hens.

- **Fowl**
  Ducks, geese, turkeys and chickens are all called poultry, and are bred in captivity to be eaten or to provide eggs, meat and feathers.

- **Old hens**
  Chickens have been domesticated since the 5th century BC and there are over 100 different varieties. Females are called hens; males are called cocks or roosters.

▷ Turkeys are a type of pheasant. There are several different species, but they all descend from the native wild turkey of North America.

- **Egg laying**
  Hens lay one or two eggs a day. To keep them laying, the eggs must be taken everyday. If not, the hens wait until they have a small collection, then sit on them, keeping them warm for about 20 days until chicks hatch.

- **Battery hens**
  Very few hens are free range. In Europe and North America, most are crowded into rows of small boxes called batteries inside a heated building where they are fed and watered, and waste and eggs are collected automatically.

- **Turkey tail**
  Male turkeys have 14–18 feathers in their tails and when courting females they spread these feathers out and raise them above their backs. All species of turkey have a 'wattle' of bare, floppy skin that hangs down from their head and neck.

- **Turkish turkeys**
  The name turkey may have come from the mistaken idea that the bird came from Turkey.

 # DATA: Farm animals

- **COW BREED**
  There are 200 or so different types of domestic cow.

- **HEAD OF SHEEP**
  There are over 680 million sheep in the world and 800 different breeds.

- **MILK PRODUCTION**
  Cows produce around 16 litres of milk a day, or 6,000 litres a year.

- **TURKEY EGGS**
  Turkey hens lay only about 12 eggs a year.

◁ The sheep was one of the first animals to be domesticated, over 10,000 years ago. Woolly sheep such as the Merino have fine wool suitable for clothing or coarse hair for carpets. Hairy sheep are bred for milk and meat. Australia, New Zealand and South America have the right climate and the right pastures for sheep rearing, and there are vast sheep farms or 'stations' here.

Tropical birds

THE TROPICS ARE HOME TO some of the world's most beautiful and spectacular birds. In the rainforests in particular there is a huge variety of colourful birds, because colour is a real asset in finding a mate. In Indonesia and Australia there are birds of paradise and lyre birds with magnificent tail feathers. In South America there are the brilliantly coloured cotingas and huge-beaked toucans. Then there are parrots, such as macaws and budgerigars, and big birds such as flamingoes and hornbills, and tiny birds such as hummingbirds.

FACTS: About weaver birds

- **Home makers**
  Weaver birds are small birds that live in the tropics of Africa and Asia. They get their name because many weave elaborate nests.

- **Nest weaving**
  Using their bills and feet they make pouch-shaped nests from plant fibres, which they suspend from tree branches, away from predators. The entrance is usually a funnel with a hole at the end, just big enough for the weaver but small enough to keep other unfriendly animals out.

- **The biggest bird nests**
  Sociable weaver birds of South Africa build big nests containing enough separate cavities for hundreds of pairs of birds under one communal roof. Each has its own entrance tunnel, complete with grass stems pointing downwards over it to help keep enemies out.

▷ Pelicans are fish-eating birds with special pouched bills which they use to scoop up fish from the water. Their pouches can hold as much as two or three times as their stomachs.

▷ The nest of the village weaver is begun by the male bird. When he has found a female willing to move in, she finishes off inside. The male then leaves her to lay her eggs while he goes off to start another nest.

▷ Like all bee-eaters, the carmine bee-eater has a long tail — the streamers are up to 12cm. Their long, downward-pointing, curved bills are perfect for catching bees on the wing. They rub the bee against a branch to remove the sting. Carmine bee-eaters of Africa often ride on the backs of other birds such as ostriches and storks, as well as grazing mammals such as antelopes and cattle, in order to pick up insects disturbed by their feet.

▶ *The Paradise whydah lives in Africa, and the male has perhaps the most spectacular tail feathers of any bird, four times as long as its body. When in flight, the whydah holds two short upper tail feathers upright while the longer ones dangle down. To attract females, it flies above her so that the long feathers wave up and down in an attractive way!*

The tail feathers of a breeding male can be as long as 28cm

◀ *The hoatzin is a large ungainly bird that lives in the forests of northern South America. It is an awkward flier so tends to glide from tree to tree. The young have two hooked claws on their wings to help them move about.*

DATA: Tropical birds

- **BIGGEST NEST**
  A South African sociable weaver bird nest can be up to 4m deep and 7.5m long.

- **OLDEST BIRD**
  The longest living captive birds are the sulphur crested cockatoos of Australia – up to 80 years.

FACTS: About parrots and cockatoos

- **Bill for nuts**
  Parrots are colourful birds of the tropics with curved bills for eating fruit and seeds and cracking nuts.

- **Parrot feet**
  Parrot feet have two toes pointing forwards and two backwards, allowing them to grip onto branches and hold food.

- **Three species**
  There are three groups of parrots — true parrots, cockatoos and lories — making 330 different species altogether. The largest is the hyacinth macaw (100cm bill to tail). The smallest is the tiny buff-faced pygmy parrot (8.4cm).

- **Mimic**
  Some parrots, such as the African grey parrot can imitate the human voice.

▲ *Like all parrots the scarlet macaw can be incredibly noisy, with a raucous, rasping caw.*

◀ *Male Andean cock-of-the-rocks are famous for their colour and their spectacular courtship routines.*

Temperate birds

BIRDS IN TEMPERATE REGIONS may not be as colourful and spectacular as those of the tropics, but there is an enormous range and variety. There are town and garden birds such as the sparrow, the magpie and the pigeon. There are woodland birds such as the nuthatch and the nightjar. There are birds that live near water too – freshwater birds such as ducks and swans, waders such as curlews and redshanks, and seabirds such as gulls and puffins. Then there are the magnificent birds of prey such as eagles, kestrels, hawks and falcons, and the night-hunting owls.

FACTS: About water birds

▷ Like many birds of wetlands, the sandhill crane has become endangered by the destruction of its habitat.

- **Waders**
  Wading birds, such as curlews and plovers, have long legs for wading through the water and long bills for probing about in the mud to look for food.

- **Waterfowl**
  Waterfowl, such as ducks, geese and swans, have webbed feet for swimming and long bendy necks for reaching into the water.

- **Seabirds**
  Many seabirds are very good divers and roam the open sea looking for food. They often lay their eggs in nesting grounds high up on the cliffs so that they are kept safely out of the reach of predators.

▷ Like many birds, the redstart feeds on insects, and has a wide beak for catching them in flight. It was originally a woodland bird, but has adapted well to environmental changes.

◁ The waxwing gets its name from the waxy red tips on some of its wing feathers. Like many seed and fruit-eating birds, it has a short pincer-like beak for cracking seeds.

▲ Common pheasants came originally from Asia, like this Monal pheasant. But they have adapted well to Britain, and are now the most widespread of all game birds, favoured by hunters.

DATA: Temperate birds

- **ANCIENT BIRD**
  The oldest known bird was a cockatoo of London Zoo, that died in 1982, aged 80.
- **SHARPEST EYES**
  The keen-eyed peregrine falcon can spot a pigeon at 8km away.

▲ *Jays are seed-eating birds that like acorns, which they bury for winter food. But they sometimes steal nestlings and eggs from the nests of other birds.*

▼ *The pigeons that swarm over many city squares are all descended from domestic pigeons, which came in turn from the wild rock dove. They are called 'feral' because they were once tame and are now wild.*

FACTS: About birds of prey

▷ *The peregrine falcon can plummet at speeds of 180kmh when diving down on prey.*

- **What are birds of prey?**
  Birds of prey are hunting birds that feed on small animals such as birds and rabbits. All have sharp, hooked bills, strong feet with talons and very good eyesight and hearing.

- **Different quarry**
  Different birds specialise in hunting different things: honey buzzards eat bees and have talons shaped for digging out nests; eagles have large talons for snatching up rabbits and squirrels; harriers eat snakes and other reptiles; ospreys specialise in catching fish such as salmon.

- **Birds under threat**
  Many birds of prey have been endangered by hunting, egg collecting and game keepers and pigeon fanciers who want to stop the birds of prey killing game birds and pigeons.

▷ *Owls hunt at night and have large, round eyes to see well in poor light, but their hearing is also so sharp they can catch prey in pitch dark by sound alone.*

Reptiles

REPTILES ARE SCALY-SKINNED CREATURES such as crocodiles, lizards and snakes. They are sometimes said to be cold-blooded. But their blood is not cold; it can be as warm as a mammal's. Mammals get their warmth by eating. Reptiles can survive on very little food, but they depend on the sun for warmth and must continually shuttle between warm and cold places to stay at the right temperature. They may spend hours basking in the sun, gaining enough energy to go hunting for food. But they depend on the sun for warmth, so cannot live in cold places.

FACTS: About snakes

- **What are snakes?**
  Snakes are thin, limbless reptiles that live mostly in warm regions. They are predators, but with no limbs; they kill their prey with poison or by constricting (squeezing) them to death.

- **Tongue scent**
  Snakes have no ears, but sense their prey from sound vibrations on the ground. They also use their tongues to smell with – but only use their eyes when close to as their eyesight is poor.

- **Snakes with bite**
  Many snakes are venomous — that is, they have a poisonous bite. Those with fangs in the front of their mouths, such as vipers and rattlesnakes, are more dangerous than back-fanged snakes — because back-fanged snakes must get a victim fully into their mouths to bite.

- **Big squeeze**
  Boas and pythons kill large victims by constriction. The snake coils itself around its victim. Each time the trapped animal breathes out the snake tightens its hold until its prey finally suffocates.

▲ The taipan is a large, poisonous snake from Australia that grows up to 3m — large for a poisonous snake. It is from the same family as the cobra — the elapids — all of which have venom in their front fangs.

▼ Like all vipers, the Gaboon viper has long fangs in the front of its mouth which hinge back into the mouth when not in use. The fangs are hollow and act as 'syringes' — injecting venom straight into the victim when the snake bites.

▲ Geckos can climb up straight walls and even run across ceilings because they have feet like suction caps. Their toes are flat with pads underneath them and these pads are covered with hundreds of tiny hooks which can grip onto flat surfaces.

▲ Turtles and tortoises are together known as chelonians and all live inside an armoured shell of bony plates. On their back is a domed 'carapace', underneath is a flat 'plastron'. Some can pull their arms, legs and head right in. They are slow moving, but withdrawing inside their shell protects them.

▶ The frilled-necked lizard of Australia may not be very big, but it makes up for its lack of size with its enormous frill. Normally, the frill hangs limp, but it spreads out up to 25cm whenever the lizard is threatened, making it look three times as large and twice as dangerous.

▼ Iguanas like the Madagascan iguana (below) are large, tropical lizards. The marine iguanas of the Galapagos are one of the very few lizards that live in the sea. They can stay under the water for up to an hour.

FACTS: About alligators

- **Crocodiles v. alligators**
  Crocodiles and alligators are large reptiles that live in warm rivers and swamps. Crocodiles have thinner snouts and a fourth tooth on the lower jaw which is visible when the mouth is shut.

- **Floating predators**
  Alligators and crocodiles are predators that lurk under the surface with just their eyes and nostrils above the water and can take prey by surprise by springing out suddenly.

▼ The alligator of the Florida Everglade swamps is now a protected animal because it was once endangered by hunters wanting its skin.

67

Amphibians

AMPHIBIANS ARE CREATURES such as frogs, toads, newts and salamanders that live part of their lives on land and part in the water. Most begin life by hatching in water from big clusters of eggs called spawn. At this stage, they are more like fish. But they soon grow legs and develop lungs for breathing air. Before long they are ready to clamber ashore, where most will spend their adult lives. Even so, they rarely stray far from water. They return to water to lay their eggs because their eggs, unlike those of reptiles, are not waterproof and so would dry out in air.

FACTS: About frogs and toads

- **Skin breathers**
  Most frogs breathe partly through their skin and so need to keep damp all the time. They are very good swimmers and, except for tree frogs, spend most of their time in or near water.

- **High jumpers**
  Neither frogs nor toads have tails as adults, but they have long, strong back legs for jumping.

- **Biggest frog**
  The largest frog is the goliath from West Africa which measures up to 80cm when stretched out and weighs up to 3kg. The smallest is a Brazilian frog — 8.5mm.

▲ Tree frogs of tropical rainforests take advantage of other moisture sources to live in the trees far from water.

- **Flying frog**
  Flying frogs are tree frogs that can glide through the air. They have sticky discs on their fingers for gripping onto branches and their hands and feet are webbed to act as airbrakes.

- **Warty toad**
  Generally, toads have drier, wartier skin than frogs and have shorter hind legs which are better for walking than jumping, unlike a frog's. Toads are also less active than frogs.

▲ Poison arrow frogs of the Amazon are brightly coloured to warn that their sweat glands contain a deadly poison – which the Indians used to smear on their arrows.

- **Baby swallower**
  The male Darwin's frog of Chile swallows the spawn left by the female and keeps it in his throat until it hatches as little tadpoles.

FACTS: About newts and salamanders

- **Lizard look-alikes**
  Newts and salamanders look a little like lizards, but they are amphibians, not reptiles like lizards, and begin life in water. Newts live in temperate climates and hibernate during the winter under logs and stones. Salamanders live in warmer areas and so do not need to hibernate.

- **Giant salamander**
  The biggest salamander of all is the giant salamander, which grows up to 1.8m long.

- **Coloured newts**
  Many male newts have bright colours and special markings during their mating season to attract females. The crested newt has a bright orange or yellow belly as well as a bumpy crest down the length of its back.

▷ *Newts are the most water-loving of all the amphibians, spending much of their lives in ponds.*

- **Egg-wrapping**
  To protect their eggs from predators, female newts wrap each egg in a leaf with their feet.

- **Fire salamander**
  Fire salamanders got their name because they shelter underneath logs and so, when in the past logs were burnt on fires, salamanders hiding underneath would come rushing out of the fire.

1. The fertilized eggs of a frog are called spawn. Each of the blobs in spawn is an egg containing an embryo, protected in a bag of jelly

2. The eggs hatch in water after a week or so into fish-like tadpoles which swim around, breathe through gills and grow rapidly

3. After 7 weeks, the tadpole begins to grow hind legs, then front legs. Soon the young froglet begins to breathe through lungs rather than gills

▷ *As they grow from eggs to adults, all amphibians, like the frog, go through a series of dramatic changes, called a metamorphosis. Each creature has its own special way of developing. But the sequence shown here for the frog is fairly typical.*

4. The froglet's legs go on growing and its tail shortens. After 14 weeks, the frog is an adult and leaves the water

Insects

INSECTS MAY BE TINY but they are by far the most numerous of all creatures. There are over a million known species, and they are found almost everywhere. Ants scurry along the ground. Bees buzz around hives. Butterflies flutter over flowers. Insects are very varied in look, but all have six legs and a body divided into three sections – head, thorax and abdomen. They also have two compound eyes with anything from six to 30,000 lenses and a variety of other sensors such as antennae (feelers) which they can use to hear, taste and smell.

FACTS: About butterflies, moths and caterpillars

- **Butterflies and moths**
  Butterflies and moths are both part of a big group of insects called Lepidoptera, which means 'scaly wings', because their wings are covered in tiny dust-like scales.

- **What's the difference?**
  Butterflies are usually brightly coloured and fly during the day. They have thin, hairless bodies and a pair of clubbed antennae. Moths tend to be drabber, because they rest during the day — on trees and dead leaves — and so must be camouflaged. They have plump, hairy bodies and straight antennae.

- **Caterpillars**
  Butterflies and moths begin life as an egg, then hatch as long thin caterpillars which eat leaves voraciously for a month.

Butterflies like the red admiral can migrate astonishing distances, as far as many birds – even crossing oceans, with the help of the wind.

- **Chrysalis and cocoon**
  When the caterpillar is ready, it spins a cocoon of silk around itself or creates a hard shell called a chrysalis. Inside, it becomes a pupa, grows wings and, amazingly, changes to an adult butterfly before emerging.

- **Nectar seeker**
  Most butterflies feed, if at all, only on nectar, the sweet juice of flowers and so spend their brief lives fluttering from bloom to bloom.

Caterpillars are fat and slow-moving, so are very vulnerable to predators. But the puss moth caterpillar can scare smaller enemies by rearing up, waving its tail and squirting formic acid.

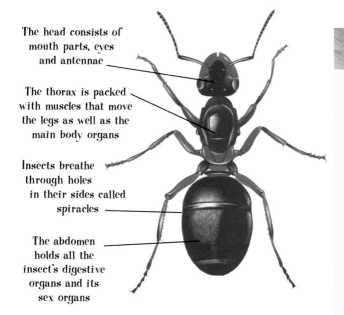

The head consists of mouth parts, eyes and antennae

The thorax is packed with muscles that move the legs as well as the main body organs

Insects breathe through holes in their sides called spiracles

The abdomen holds all the insect's digestive organs and its sex organs

△ Insects look very different from other animals. Not only are their bodies split into three sections, but they have no bones. Instead, they have a rigid shell or 'exoskeleton', made of a tough substance called chitin.

FACTS: About bees

- **Bee hive**
  Bees live together in large numbers in hives or nests. In each colony there is one queen, many female workers and a few drones (males).

- **Queen bee**
  Only the queen can lay eggs — up to 1,000 a day. Drones exist only to mate with the queen, after which they die.

- **Worker bee**
  Workers collect pollen and nectar from flowers and bring it to the nest. Pollen is fed to grubs and nectar is used for honey.

▷ A honeybee's main protection is the sting in its tail. Its bright yellow and black stripes are a warning.

◁ Dragonflies are large, fast-flying insects that can dart at up to 60kmh. Their four wings move independently of one another and make a rattling sound. They can also fly backwards.

DATA: Insects

- **LONGEST INSECT**
  The world's longest insect is the giant stick insect of Borneo which grows up to 33cm long.

- **SMALLEST INSECT**
  The world's smallest is the fairy fly, just 0.2mm long.

- **AN ANT'S STRENGTH**
  An ant can lift 50 times its own weight – that is like you lifting a lorry!

△ Termites are insects that live in huge colonies in the tropics. Together, they build huge mounds to live in out of dust and saliva, complete with air conditioning. Some termite mounds can be 9m tall.

Key facts: Animals

Kingdoms

1. Monerans
Simple single cell organisms with no nucleus, eg. bacteria.
2. Protista
Mostly single cell organisms with a nucleus, eg. amoebas.
3. Fungi
Multi-celled organisms that feed on living or dead organic matter, e.g. moulds.
4. Plantae
Multi-celled organisms such as trees, plants and grasses.
5. Animalia
Animals — multi-celled organisms which must find food and can move around.

The animal kingdom:
- Vertebrates
  Mammals
  Birds
  Amphibians
  Reptiles
  Jawless fish
  Sea squirts
  Sharks and rays
  Bony fish
- Invertebrates
  Echinoderms
  Arthropods
  Velvetworms, lampshells etc.
  Worms of all kinds
  Sponges
  Cnidaria
  Molluscs

Animal classification

Classification of a lion:

Kingdom
Animalia
Multi-celled organisms which cannot make their own food.
Phylum
Chordate
Animals that have a single nerve cord at some stage during their life.
Class
Mammal
Animals that suckle their young on milk and have hair or fur.
Order
Carnivore
Land mammals adapted to hunting.

Family
Cats
Have sharp, retractable front claws.
Genus
Big cats
Includes five species — lions, tigers, leopards, snow leopards and jaguars.
Species
Lion

Males, females and babies

Animal	Male	Female	Young
Antelope	Buck	Doe	Kid
Bobcat	Tom	Lioness	Kitten
Buffalo	Bull	Cow	Calf
Camel	Bull	Cow	Calf
Caribou	Stag	Doe	Fawn
Duck	Drake	Duck	Duckling
Fish	Cock	Hen	Fry
Goat	Billygoat	Nannygoat	Kid
Goose	Gander	Goose	Gosling
Seal	Bull	Cow	Pup
Swan	Cob	Pen	Cygnet
Weasel	Boar	Cow	Kit

Animal habitats

Freshwater lakes
- otter, water vole, harvest mouse
- reed warbler, heron, kingfisher, marsh harrier, coot
- frog, toad, newt
- dragonfly, pondskater, waterboatman, mayfly
- stickleback, trench, pike, bream

Tundra and Arctic
- polar bear, Arctic fox, Arctic hare, grey wolf, vole, ermine, lemming, musk ox, caribou
- eagle, grouse, plover, goose, snowy owl
- mosquito

Mountains
- ibex, chamois deer, yak, llama, vicuna, puma, snow leopard, lynx, chinchilla, marmot
- eagle, condor, lammergeier
- ice worm

Tropical grasslands
- giraffe, zebra, antelope, lion, leopard, cheetah, elephant, water buffalo, mongoose, hyena, jackal
- ostrich, marabou stork, oxpecker, weaver bird, secretary bird, vulture
- Eastern brown snake, red-bellied snake
- dung beetle, termite, locust

Temperate grasslands
- saiga antelope, pronghorn antelope, bison, prairie dog, mole rat, coyote, fox
- rhea, guanaco, buzzard
- grass snake, lizard
- grasshopper, fly

Tropical forests
- monkey, leopard, shrew, sloth, coati, opossum, okapi, tamandua, jaguar
- macaw, parrot, toucan, hummingbird, jacamar
- viper, anaconda, python, tree frog, iguana, crocodile, turtle
- morpho butterfly, hunting spider, ant

Temperate forests
- squirrel, skunk, badger, mouse, raccoon, hedgehog, chipmunk, beaver, rabbit, fox, deer, bear, wolf, wild boar
- warbler, tit, woodpecker, woodcock, jay, owl
- salamander, slug
- ant, purple emperor butterfly, moth, beetle, earthworm, snail, centipede

Deserts
- camel, addax, fennec fox, long-eared jackrabbit, kangaroo rat, gundi, jerboa
- roadrunner, hummingbird, vulture, nighthawk, burrowing owl, sand grouse
- spiny lizard, gila monster, rattlesnake, gecko, thorny devil, tortoise
- scorpion, antlion, spider

Seashore
- anenome, barnacle, mussle, starfish, crab, sea cucumber, cockle, lugworm, sea urchin, scallop, limpet
- gull, tern, gannet, pelican

Oceans
- Surface waters: seal, porpoise, shark, mackerel, jellyfish, turtle, sea horse
- Mid-ocean: squid, octopus, swordfish, hatchet fish, lanternfish, flatfish
- Deep sea: ray, gulper eel, angler fish, giant squid, sperm whale

Key facts: Animals

Birds

- **The biggest bird**
  The biggest bird is the ostrich which can grow up to 2.7m tall.
- **The smallest bird**
  The smallest bird is the bee hummingbird which is just 57mm long.
- **The biggest flying bird**
  The biggest flying bird is the mute swan which can weigh up to 22.5kg.
- **The biggest bird of prey**
  The Andean condor can weigh 11kg or more.
- **The fastest flier**
  The fastest flier is the peregrine falcon which can dive at up to 30kmh.
- **The oldest bird**
  Cocky the cockatoo of London Zoo was over 80 when he died in 1982.

- **The longest journey**
  A common tern flew 22,530km from Russia down through the Atlantic over Africa and the Indian Ocean to Australia.
- **The most time in the air**
  No bird spends more time flying than the sooty tern which can remain in the air for 3–10 years.
- **The biggest egg**
  The biggest egg is the ostrich egg which can grow up to 20cm across.
- **The highest flier**
  The highest flight was by a Ruppell's vulture which hit a plane at 11,277m.
- **The fastest swimmer**
  A gentoo penguin reaches 27 kmh.

Sea creatures

- **The smallest fish**
  The smallest fish is the Indo-Pacific dwarf goby which is only 12–19mm long.
- **The largest fish**
  The largest fish is the whale shark which can grow over 12m long.
- **The fastest fish**
  The fastest fish is the sailfish which can travel at up to 109kmh.
- **The oldest fish**
  The whale shark can live to over 70 years.
- **The deadliest jellyfish**
  The deadly Australian sea wasp can kill a man in just one minute.

- **The noisiest animal**
  The noisiest animal is the blue whale. Its sounds can be detected from as far away as 830km.
- **The smallest crab**
  The smallest crab is the pea crab, which really is as small as a pea.
- **The largest turtle**
  The largest turtle is the Pacific leatherback which grows up to 2.13m long.
- **The longest journey**
  European eels travel 7,500km on their spawning migration from the Baltic to the Sargasso Sea.

Mammals

- **The biggest mammal**
  The biggest mammal is the blue whale which can grow up to 33m long and weigh up to 190 tonnes.
- **The biggest land mammal**
  The biggest land mammal is the African bush elephant which can grow up to 4m tall and weigh up to 12 tonnes.
- **The tallest mammal**
  The tallest mammal is the giraffe which can grow over 5.5m tall.
- **The smallest mammal**
  The smallest mammal is the bumblebee bat of Thailand which weighs under 2g.
- **The smallest land mammal**
  The smallest land mammal is the Savi's pygmy which is under 50mm long.
- **The fastest sprinting land mammal**
  The fastest land mammal is the cheetah which can reach 100kmh for short bursts.
- **The fastest running land mammal**
  The fastest running land mammal over a sustained distance is the North American pronghorn antelope, which can keep up 56kmh for over 6km.
- **The fastest marine mammal**
  The fastest swimming mammal is the killer whale which can reach 55kmh.
- **The highest jumper**
  The highest jumping animals are pumas and leopards which can jump over 5m into trees.
- **The oldest mammal**
  The oldest mammal (apart from humans, of course) is the elephant which can live more than 70 years.

Reptiles

- **The largest reptile**
  The largest reptile is the estuarine crocodile of SE Asia which can grow to more than 6m in length.
- **The biggest lizard**
  The biggest lizard is the komodo dragon which averages 2.25m in length.
- **The biggest amphibian**
  The biggest amphibian is the Chinese giant salamander which is over 1m long.
- **The longest snake**
  The longest snake may be the reticulated python which can grow over 9m long.
- **The most poisonous snake**
  The most poisonous snake is the marine cobra of the western Pacific.

Insects

- **The heaviest insects**
  The heaviest insects are the goliath beetles of Africa at up to 100g.
- **The longest insect**
  The longest insects are stick insects which can grow up to 500mm long.
- **The fastest flier**
  The Australian dragonfly can reach 60kmh.
- **The largest butterfly**
  The Queen Alexandra's birdwing of Papua New Guinea can be up to 300mm across.
- **The loudest insect**
  Male cicadas (like crickets) rub their abdomens so loud they can be heard from 400m away.

Quiz: Animals

1. What is the world's smallest bird?

   bee humingbird

2. What is the smallest land mammal?

3. What's a beaver's home called?

4. What is a margay?

5. What bird makes the longest migration?

6. What sea mammals have two long tusks?

7. What do seals mainly eat?

8. What do whales have on the tops of their heads?

9. Which is the largest meat-eater in the Arctic?

10. Which animal can sprint the fastest?

11. What is a group of lions called?

12. What is the world's biggest mammal?

13. What animal has a horn on the end of its snout?

14. How can you tell an adult male lion from a female?

15. Which is the biggest bird of prey?

16. What are the claws of a bird of prey called?

17. The sooty tern can fly non-stop for 10 years: true or false?

18. Crocodiles, lizards and snakes are all kinds of what?

19. The male Darwin's frog swallows the spawn laid by the female and keeps it in its throat until it hatches into little tadpoles: true or false?

20. Can a butterfly fly across an ocean?

Answers:

1. The bee hummingbird (at just 57mm long)
2. Savi's pygmy shrew
3. A lodge
4. One of the smaller 'big cats'
5. Common tern
6. Walrus
7. Mainly fish
8. A blowhole, for breathing out
9. The polar bear
10. The cheetah, reaching speeds of up to 100kph
11. A pride
12. The blue whale
13. A rhinoceros
14. An adult male has a big mane; a lioness does not
15. The Andean condor
16. Talons
17. True
18. Reptiles
19. True
20. Yes

PLANTS

Plants

THERE ARE OVER 250,000 different kinds of plant, ranging from tiny plankton barely visible under a microscope to giant trees hundreds of metres tall, the world's largest living things. They grow almost everywhere – on land and in the sea, on plains and on mountaintops, even in deserts and snowy wastes. Indeed, 40% of the world's land is covered by trees and grass. What makes plants very different from animals is that they do not move around and have no need of senses (or a brain) because they can make their own food from sunlight.

FACTS: About stems

- **The plant stem**
  The stem supports the plant's flowers and leaves. It is also a pipe to take water, minerals and food up and down between the roots and the leaves. Water goes up from the roots via tubes called xylem. Food goes down from the leaves in tubes called phloem.

- **Woody and herbaceous**
  Many plants have stems that are green and bendy. They are called herbaceous plants, because many are herbs such as parsley. Woody plants such as trees have stiff stems or trunks covered in bark.

▶ *Bamboo is an unusual plant. It is a kind of grass and starts off with a soft, bendy, herbaceous stem. But as it grows, very rapidly, the stem becomes hard, tough and woody.*

FACTS: About leaves

- **Sun traps**
  Leaves are a plant's solar cells and catch the light to make the food the plant needs to grow. Most are broad and flat to catch as much sun as possible.

- **Stalk and blade**
  Each leaf is attached to the stem by a small stalk called a petiole. The flat part of the leaf is called the blade.

- **Simple and compound**
  Some leaves, such as maple leaves, are called simple leaves because they have only one blade. Other leaves, such as those of the walnut and willow, are called compound because they have a number of blades on the same stalk.

- **Biggest leaves**
  The biggest leaves belong to the raffia palm tree, which can grow up to 20m long.

▶ *The lines on leaves are veins which not only provide a frame to support the leaf, but carry water in and the food the leaf makes out.*

Gymnosperm:
pine tree

Angiosperm:
edelweiss

◀ The first plants to grow on land were plants such as fungi and lichen which grow from tiny cells called spores. But most plants today grow not from spores but seeds. Unlike the more primitive spore-making plants, seed-making plants have stems, leaves, and often roots and flowers. Seed-making plants are divided into gymnosperms which have cones, and angiosperms which bear flowers.

FACTS: About photosynthesis

◀ Leaves are made up from lots of tiny parcels called cells. The wall is made of a tough material called cellulose. Inside are bundles called chloroplasts, which are the plant's solar energy converters.

- **Food making**
  Plants make their food by absorbing sunlight in a process called photosynthesis. The sun gives the plant energy to change carbon dioxide from the air, and hydrogen from water, into food.

- **Green packages**
  Photosynthesis occurs in tiny packages in leaf cells called chloroplasts. These contain a green substance called chlorophyll, which makes leaves green. It is this that soaks up the sun.

▶ In photosynthesis, chlorophyll in the leaves uses the sun's energy to turn carbon dioxide from the air and hydrogen from water into sugars which the plant uses as fuel for growth.

Carbon dioxide is absorbed through pores in the leaves called stomata

When the sun shines, chlorophyll in the leaves soaks up the energy to split water into oxygen and hydrogen

In the leaves hydrogen joins with carbon dioxide to make sugar

The remaining oxygen goes out into the air. This is called respiration

Water and minerals are drawn up through the stem

Minerals are drawn from the soil

Water is drawn up through the roots

81

Roots and bulbs

THE GREEN AND COLOURFUL PARTS of a plant are the leaves and flowers you see above the ground – but there is more to a plant beneath the surface. This is where the plant's roots are, growing down into soil or water. Roots not only hold the plant in place, anchoring it in the soil, but also draw up the water and minerals that the plant needs to grow. In some plants, such as beetroots, the roots also act as a food store. Sometimes, new plants can grow, or plants that die back can regrow, from the parts below ground, which form bulbs, corms, rhizomes and tubers.

FACTS: About roots

▲ *Root vegetables are vegetables that grow underground. But not all of them are really roots. Carrots and beetroot are true roots, but potatoes are tubers, which are underground stems, and onions are bulbs, which are underground leaves.*

- **Growing plant**
  When a plant begins to grow, the seed sends out a single primary root. This quickly branches out into secondary roots. The tips of these are protected by a root cap as they probe out through the soil.

- **Taproots**
  Some plants have just one very large root, with only a few very fine roots sprouting off it. The large root is called a taproot.

- **Fibrous roots**
  Some plants, such as grasses, have lots of fine roots spreading out in a dense mat. These are called fibrous roots. Some rye grasses grow 12,000km of roots in just a cubic metre of soil.

- **Root hairs**
  Every root has very fine 'root hairs' branching off it. These hairs are very good at soaking up water and minerals from the soil.

- **Parasitic roots**
  Parasitic plants are unable to take up water and minerals from the soil themselves. Instead they draw their food from other plants. Mistletoe, for instance, wraps its roots around apple trees.

- **Climbing roots**
  Some climbing plants, like ivy, don't only have roots underground, but on the stem too. These stem roots serve mainly to hold the plant on to trees, walls and fences.

- **Deepest roots**
  The roots of a wild fig tree in Transvaal, South Africa go down 120m into the ground. An elm tree seen growing in Largs, Scotland, had roots 110m deep.

FACTS: About bulbs, corms, rhizomes and tubers

- **New from old**
  Some plants grow only once from a seed. But many perennials can die back then grow anew again and again from parts of a root or stem. This is called vegetative propagation.

- **Rhizomes**
  Plants such as irises sprout from thick stems called rhizomes that grow sideways beneath the ground.

- **Tubers**
  Sometimes, the end of a rhizome swells into lumps called tubers. Potatoes are tubers.

- **Corms**
  Flowers such as crocuses grow from the bulbous base to their stem, called a corm.

Corm

Tuber

Bulb

Rhizome

▲ To survive the winter, many plants die back to leave nothing visible above the ground. But the plant stays alive in the form of a corm, tuber, bulb or rhizome. All of these are 'storage organs', providing food to sustain the plant through the winter and to feed new shoots when they re-emerge the following spring.

- **Bulbs**
  Bulbs, such as onions, look like corms, but they are actually made of leaf parts rather than the stem, which is why the onion has layers.

- **Food stores**
  Plants such as lupins grow in a ring around the outside of an old stem as the stem gets older and grows wider.

FACTS: About runners and suckers

◀ Strawberry plants are plants that spread by growing runners — that is, long stems that creep over the ground. Here and there along the stem it puts down new roots and a new plant grows.

Strawberry runners

- **Creeping stems**
  Some plants, such as roses, propagate (grow new plants) not from seeds or bulbs, corms, rhizomes or tubers, but from long thin stems that creep over the ground (runners) or under it (suckers).

- **Buried leaves**
  With some plants, like begonias, new plants can grow from broken leaves that get embedded in the soil.

Flowers, seeds & fruits

MOST OF THE WORLD'S PLANTS are flowers. Not only garden and wild flowers, but many trees and every herb, shrub, grain, fruit and vegetable is a flowering plant or 'angiosperm'. The blooms may not all be as big and beautiful as those of a rose, but all flowering plants have flowers, and all serve a purpose. Flowers are not just for show – they are sexual, just like us, and contain male parts which make the pollen to fertilize the eggs or 'ovules' made by female parts. Only when these come together can flowers create the fruits and seeds from which new plants will grow.

FACTS: About seeds and fruits

- **Seeds**
  Seeds are the tiny packages from which new plants grow. A hard shell or 'kernel' holds not only the new plant in embryo, but all the food it needs to nourish it.

- **What is a fruit?**
  When scientists talk of fruit they don't just mean apples and pears, but the part of a flower that protects the seed as it ripens and helps spread it. A flower's eggs grow inside its ovaries. Once the eggs are fertilized and turned into seeds, the ovary swells around it into a fruit.

- **Juicy fruits**
  Fruits are often juicy and sweet when ripe so that animals are tempted to eat them. The seeds are then spread in the animals' droppings.

◄ The pips inside each grape are seeds from which new grape vines might grow.

◄ Even though they are often very small, like this bottlebrush of Australia, most trees have flowers.

- **Plums and cherries**
  Fruits such as plums are called 'drupes'. They have a fleshy outside and a hard kernel or stone inside protecting the seeds. The stone may be too big for animals to swallow so they eat just the flesh, but the seeds still get spread.

- **False fruits**
  Some fruits are called false fruits because they are made from more than just the ovary of the flower. Apples and pears, for example, have the ovary as their core, but their fleshy parts are actually swollen stalk.

- **Legumes**
  Peas, beans and other legumes are soft, dry fruits held in a case called a pod.

▶ Poppies are 'annuals' and flower, scatter their seeds and die in just one year. Buds appear in early summer, then open up as it gets warmer, releasing a flower which is fully grown by midsummer. Once pollinated, their petals wither and fall off, leaving a seed capsule. By autumn, the capsule has dried and developed holes, and the ripe seeds can be shaken out by the wind.

1. The fully formed flower is packed inside a bud, enclosed by the green 'sepals'

2. Once the weather is warm enough, the bud begins to open

3. The sepals open wider and the petals grow outwards and backwards

4. The poppy is now fully grown and ready to attract insects. Poppy flowers always have four petals

5. After pollination, the petals fall away, leaving a seed capsule

6. By autumn, small holes appear at the top of the dry capsule so seeds can be shaken out

FACTS: About spreading plants

▶ Pollen are the male germ cells which must reach the eggs to fertilize them. They are microscopically small and some are spread by sticking to the legs and bodies of insects drawn to the flower's nectar.

• Scattered far and wide
Plants can't move, but they can spread their pollen and seeds over a wide area. Only a few seeds will grow, so plants usually produce large numbers to ensure their survival.

• Seed spreading
Some seeds are so tiny that they are easily carried by the wind. Others have hooks or hairs on them so that they catch on the fur of passing animals.

Garden & wildflowers

ALL FLOWERS WERE WILD ONCE but through history gardeners have adapted them to the garden by selecting seeds and grafting plants together to bring out particular qualities. Their efforts have created a huge range of beautiful new plants, including roses, carnations, chrysanthemums, tulips and many more. There are now more than a million kinds of garden flower, while wildflowers are becoming rare as human activity restricts the places where they can grow. Many wildflowers, such as the lady's slipper orchid, are now in danger of becoming extinct.

FACTS: Garden flowers

- **Big and bold**
  On the whole, garden flowers have much bigger flowers in bolder colours than their wild cousins. The wild dog rose has tiny pale pink or white blooms. Garden roses have big blooms in strong colours, from deep red to blue.

- **Cut flowers**
  Once cut flowers could only be bought in the right season. Now they are grown in warm places all year round such as Colombia and flown in chilled conditions to bring them fresh to local shops in under two days.

▼ *An enormous range of cut flowers can now be bought all year round.*

FACTS: Wild flowers

▶ *The edelweiss survives because it can grow at very high altitude in the Alps, sprouting out from cracks in the rocks. This is because its leaves and blooms are covered in a coat of woolly hairs that protect it from the cold.*

- **Meadows and woodlands**
  Every kind of place has its own kind of wild flower. On heathlands, flowers such as bell-heather, gorse and scarlet pimpernel grow. In meadows, tiny buttercups, daisies, clover and ragged robin grow in the grass. In woodlands, flowers like bluebells, primroses and celandines grow. By the sea, sea campion and thrift grow on the rocks, and birdsfoot trefoil on grassy clifftops.

- **Protected flowers**
  Some wildflowers are now so rare that the few survivors must be protected by law. This is true of many orchids.

FACTS: About perennials & biennials

▲ The giant sunflower is a perennial. It is a native of Peru but is now grown in many places, both for its big yellow flowers and for its seeds which give cooking oil.

- **Annuals**
  Annuals are plants such as delphiniums that grow from seeds, flower, disperse their seeds and die in a single growing season.

- **Biennials**
  Biennials live for two years. In the first, the plant grows leaves on a bulb or taproot which sustains it with food through the winter. It flowers in the second summer.

- **Perennials**
  Perennials such as wallflowers and chrysanthemums live several years, surviving through the winter on underground food stores such as bulbs.

- **Ephemerals**
  Ephemerals such as groundsel are short-lived plants that grow from seed, bloom and die within a few weeks.

▼ Flowers probably evolved their colourful blooms and beautiful scents to attract the insects they rely on for pollination. But the efforts of gardeners over the centuries have added many new and often spectacular blooms to those created by natural evolution, including roses, tulips, delphiniums, and many more. Many of these new flowers no longer rely on insects for pollination, but are pollinated by humans.

Lupin
Carnation
Tulip
Michaelmas daisy
Rose
Soapwort
Rosebay willowherb
Bluebell
Poppy
Scarlet pimpernel

How trees grow

ALTHOUGH SOME DWARF WILLOWS grow just a few centimetres high, trees are generally the largest of all plants. Indeed the giant redwood tree is the biggest of all living things. Trees can grow big because they don't have soft, green 'herbaceous' stems like other plants; they have stiff, brown, woody stems, covered in protective bark, that can grow tall and support an enormous weight of leaves. With most trees, there is a single, thick central stem – the trunk – and leaves and side branches only grow some way off the ground – so they are well out of the reach of most browsing animals.

FACTS: About tree trunks

▲ Slicing through a tree's trunk can reveal a lot about its history – its age, the rate at which it has grown and the conditions it has faced over the years.

- **Inside the trunk**
  The centre of a trunk is the dead 'heartwood'. The living part is the middle – the 'sapwood' and the 'cambium'. Outside is a protective layer of bark.

- **Tree rings**
  Each ring inside the trunk represents a year's growth. Rings close together indicate slow growth; rings far apart indicate rapid growth.

FACTS: About seeds

- **Seed production**
  Because only a small portion of their seeds survive, most trees produce thousands each year.

- **Seed dispersal**
  The seeds of many trees are dispersed by wind, so are shaped to become airborne easily — maple tree seeds are encased in a pair of flat wings, while willow seeds are shaped like tiny parachutes.

▼ Many trees have seeds that are spread by the wind. The eucalyptus trees of Australia are among the many which have long helicopter-like wings on which they can flutter long distances before they land.

▶ Timber is either hardwood, from broad-leaved trees, or softwood, from conifers. Softwood trees are much faster growing (about 10m every 30 years) and are grown in huge numbers on plantations in places like the Rocky Mountains, North America (right). Because they grow faster, these trees provide softer wood. Softwoods are mostly used for making cheap furniture, paper and for building. Hardwoods are used for more expensive furniture and shipbuilding.

◀ Cedars have smooth, upright cones which are made up of lots of closely packed scales, each attached to two seeds. Over a few years these scales gradually break off the cones and fall to the ground, taking their seeds with them.

- **Seed cones**
  The seeds of conifers develop inside hard, protective cones until they are ready.

- **Catkins**
  Oak trees produce male flowers called catkins — long clusters that hang from the branches and release pollen into the air. When the pollen lands on the ovaries of female flowers and fertilizes them, the ovaries develop into acorns.

- **Nuts and berries**
  Some trees have seeds growing inside soft, fleshy fruits, such as berries. Others have them growing inside hard shells, such as acorns and walnuts.

DATA: Trees

- **THE BIGGEST TREE**
  The biggest tree in the world is 'General Sherman', a giant sequoia in California – 83m tall and 25m round.

- **THE FASTEST GROWING TREES**
  The fastest growing tree is the Albizia falcata, a tropical pea tree which can grow 10m in 13 months.

- **THE LONGEST LIVING TREE**
  The oldest surviving tree was a bristlecone pine in Nevada, USA, which had lived for 5,100 years.

- **THE LONGEST LIVING SPECIES**
  The oldest surviving species of tree is thought to be the maidenhair tree of China, which first appeared over 160 million years ago.

Deciduous trees

DECIDUOUS TREES are trees that lose their leaves at some time during the year, usually to cut down their need for water. In cool regions, they lose them in winter because water is hard to come by when groundwater is frozen. In warm regions, they lose them in the summer when the soil dries out quickly. All deciduous trees are flowering plants (see page 84) and have broad, flat leaves, which is why they are also known as broad-leaved trees – although there are also evergreen broad-leaved trees. Broad-leaved trees include deciduous trees such as ash and chestnut, evergreen trees such as holly, and palm trees.

FACTS: About palm trees

- **Long leaves**
  Palm trees have thick, tough leaves that help them survive in hot places. There are about 2,800 species, some with leaves as long as 12m and as wide as 2.5m.

- **No branches**
  Palms have no branches. The leaves grow directly out from the trunk.

▶ *The leaves, stems and fruit of palm trees provide lots of useful products, ranging from baskets, furniture, food and oil. Even soap.*

▼ *In spring, the buds of new leaves shoot on the trees, and slowly open. Flowers appear on the tree, too, and fruit trees blossom. Because plenty of sunlight can still filter down to the ground through the thin canopy of leaves, woodland flowers such as bluebells bloom beneath the trees.*

▼ *In summer, the leaves on the trees are fully grown, providing a sheltered home for a wide variety of different animals and plants. The dense foliage keeps the woodland beneath at an even temperature — nights are warmer and days are cooler here than out in the open.*

FACTS: About deciduous trees

- **Tree life**
  Oaks and other trees can live up to 500 years. Some elms which reproduce from suckers never really die at all because the trees are constantly renewing themselves, creating a whole grove of their offshoots.

- **Fallen trees**
  Every now and then, trees die and fall over. As they crash to the floor, they open up the woodland floor to the sky, creating a glade where new trees and other plants thrive.

▲ *Deciduous forests once covered the whole of Europe and eastern North America, but now only fragments of these remain.*

- **Oak trees**
  There are 450 species of oak tree, some deciduous, some evergreen. But all grow from acorns.

- **Dutch elm disease**
  Elm trees were once common in northern Europe, but many have been killed by Dutch elm disease — a fungus whose spores are spread by beetles that live in the bark.

- **Coppicing**
  Many woodlands have long been managed by foresters. Trees such as willows are cut off at the trunk or 'coppiced'. The new straight shoots that grow from the top make 'withies', good for basketmaking.

▼ *By autumn, the days are getting colder and there is less water available. To survive, the trees must prepare to lose their leaves. The chlorophyll which makes the leaves green starts to break down and sugars in the leaves gradually turn them brown, red or orange.*

▼ *As winter approaches the trees get ready to close down altogether. The leaves that changed colour in the autumn start to drop off, leaving the trees bare and dormant. During this time, though, winter buds develop, containing new leaves which will burst open the following spring.*

Conifers and cycads

CONIFERS, AND THEIR TROPICAL RELATIVES cycads and gingkos, are among the oldest of all kinds of plants. They first appeared over 300 million years ago, long before the age of dinosaurs. Conifers, cycads and gingkos are all called gymnosperms, and make their seeds in cones. Conifers are tall, mostly evergreen trees that generally grow in cool and mountainous regions. A few cypresses are the only tropical conifers. Cycads, however, are tropical trees that look like stubby palm trees. Gingkos or maidenhair trees are tall trees with fan-shaped leaves that grow only in eastern China.

FACTS: About coniferous forests

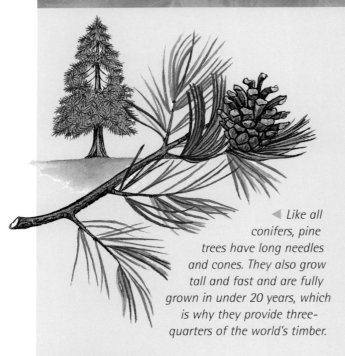

◄ Like all conifers, pine trees have long needles and cones. They also grow tall and fast and are fully grown in under 20 years, which is why they provide three-quarters of the world's timber.

• **Cold resistance**
Conifers are able to survive in cold areas with little water because instead of leaves they have thin waxy needles that shed snow easily and lose very little water. (Water cannot be used by trees when it is frozen.) Their tall, narrow shape helps shed snow too.

• **Evergreen**
Nearly all conifers are evergreen, which means that their leaves stay on all year round. Larches are an exception — their needles fall off in autumn.

• **Plantations**
In various cold regions of the world conifers are grown in narrowly planted rows on massive plantations to provide timber. They are fast growing and can also survive on soil which is too poor for other crops.

• **Life in a coniferous forest**
Coniferous forests are usually quite dense and dark, and so there is much less other plant life beneath the trees than there is in a deciduous forest (see page 90) — usually just fungi, ferns and lichen.

• **Pine family**
Pines make up the largest family of conifers. This includes almost 100 different species, such as the Scots pine, Corsican pine and the Loblolly pine.

• **Boreal forest**
The most extensive coniferous forests are found in the colder, northern parts of the world — mostly North America, Scandinavia and Siberia.

• **Tree mix**
Most coniferous forests are made up of conifers like pines, spruces and firs.

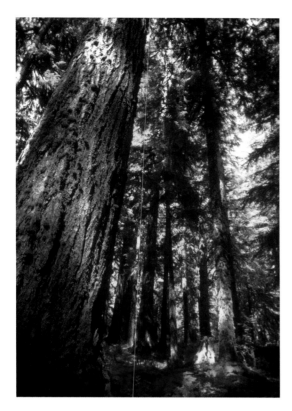

▲ *The giant redwood or sequoia trees of Sierra Nevada in California are the world's largest living things, growing 100m or more tall. Some are among the oldest too. There are redwoods here that date back to before the days of the Ancient Egyptians, 4,000 years ago.*

DATA: Big, old trees

- **THE TALLEST LIVING TREE**
  The tallest tree in the world is a coast redwood in Humboldt Redwoods State Park, California, USA – 112.7m.

- **THE OLDEST LIVING TREE**
  Is a 5,100 year old bristlecone pine in California's White Mts.

- **THE BIGGEST FOREST**
  Is in Siberia – over 17 million square kilometres.

FACTS: Seeds and cones

- **Cone-bearers**
  Instead of flowers, conifers and cycads have male and female cones which produce and carry seeds.

- **Male cones**
  The smaller male cones grow in clusters and produce pollen grains which travel on the wind to fertilize the female cones.

- **Female cones**
  Once fertilized, female cones may take as long as three years to develop their seeds.

- **Female scales**
  Each scale of the female cone has one or more seeds attached to it. As they develop they are protected within the hard cone. When they are ready, the scales open up and either release the seeds or fall away from the cone, taking the seeds with them.

▲ *Cones are very sensitive to changes in the dampness of the air. In dry weather, the scales shrivel and stand out stiffly. When it is damper, they absorb the moisture and close up neatly again.*

Mosses and ferns

NOT ALL PLANTS GROW FROM SEEDS. The very first plants to grow on land some 400 million years ago grew from tiny, dust-like cells called spores. These ancient plants, including mosses, liverworts, club mosses, horsetails and ferns, still survive today, though none of them ever grows as big as they did in the time before seed-bearing plants appeared some 200 million years ago. They love damp, shady places, and are often seen carpeting rocks along streams and growing all over trees in moist woodlands and steamy tropical rainforests - sometimes far above the ground.

FACTS: About ferns

- **Roots, leaves and stems**
  Unlike mosses, ferns are 'pteridophytes' or featherplants and have roots and leaves, and veins to take food and water up and down inside the stem. Fern leaves are called fronds.

- **Tree ferns**
  Tree ferns are big ferns that can grow up to 25m tall, and they are abundant in moist tropical rainforests. They have no branches, and the fronds grow in a crown from the top of the trunk.

- **Passenger plants**
  Some ferns, such as bird's-nest fern and stag's horn fern, grow on other plants without harming them. They get their moisture by collecting dripping rainwater.

- **Horsetails**
  Horsetails are similar to ferns, but they belong to a group called sphenophytes. Although nowadays most are small, these plants grew more than 30m tall in the Carboniferous Period 300–355 million years ago.

▶ *Ferns grow from spores made on the underside of their leaves. The spores form a prothallus, which creates the embryo for a new fern to grow from.*

Sporangia are where the fern makes spores

In each sori, there are sacs called sporangia

On the underside of leaves are balls called sori

The root and stem grow to form a new fern frond

A new root and stem grow and the prothallus dies away

FACTS: About moss

- **Moss**
  Mosses and liverworts make up a group of their own called bryophytes. They form in thin cushions on walls, rocks and old logs and have no true roots so they have to draw their moisture from the air through their stems and tiny threads called rhizoids. This is why they like damp places such as river banks.

- **Sponges**
  Sphagnum moss lives in bogs and can soak up to 25 times its own weight in water. It is the main constituent in peat bogs in Ireland and Scotland.

- **New moss**
  Moss spores make male and female cells, which swim together to create the embryo for a new moss.

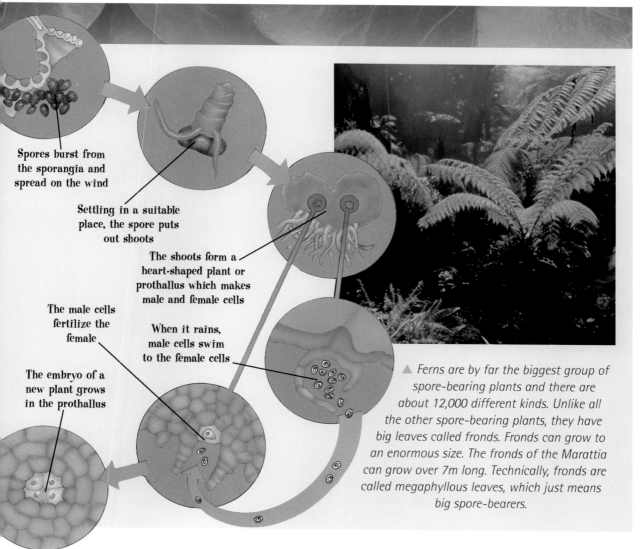

Spores burst from the sporangia and spread on the wind

Settling in a suitable place, the spore puts out shoots

The shoots form a heart-shaped plant or prothallus which makes male and female cells

The male cells fertilize the female

When it rains, male cells swim to the female cells

The embryo of a new plant grows in the prothallus

▲ Ferns are by far the biggest group of spore-bearing plants and there are about 12,000 different kinds. Unlike all the other spore-bearing plants, they have big leaves called fronds. Fronds can grow to an enormous size. The fronds of the Marattia can grow over 7m long. Technically, fronds are called megaphyllous leaves, which just means big spore-bearers.

Fungi and mushrooms

FUNGI AND MUSHROOMS grow in the ground like plants, but they are not plants at all. Fungi and mushrooms, along with toadstools, yeast, mildew and mould (like the mould on bread), all belong to a special group of organisms called Myceteae. Unlike plants, fungi have no green chlorophyll, so cannot make their own food. So they have to get their food in other ways. Many fungi are parasites, which means they feed off living animals, plants and other organisms. Others are saprophytes, which means they live off the remains of dead plants and animals.

▶ Fungi are both good and bad for us. Some kinds of fungi, such as mushrooms and cheese mould, are good to eat, but others are deadly poisonous. Some grow on plants and animals and make them ill, such as the aspergillus mould. Others provide antibiotic drugs. Yeast helps bread rise and beer ferment.

Destroying angel

Fly agaric

Honey fungus

FACTS: About parasites

▲ Fungi live off other organisms. These fungi are growing on a tree, clinging on with hundreds of cotton-like threads called hyphae, which digest and absorb materials from the tree.

• **Chemical rotters**
Fungi rot the organism they are feeding on by sending out special chemicals called enzymes, which break down plant and animal cells.

• **Food source**
Fungi absorb food from the rotting organism.

• **Blue cheese**
The enzymes released by mould are what give blue cheese its flavour — and make bread mould toxic.

Puffball

FACTS: What fungi are made of

- **Spreading threads**
Fungi are made of cotton-like threads called hyphae which spread out in a tangled mass through the soil — or into the tissues of the plant or animal the fungi are living on.

◀ Sometimes, hyphae (pronounced hi-fi) bundle together to form what are called fruiting bodies — such as mushrooms and toadstools. But they can also make tiny pinheads, such as the mould on rotting fruit.

Shaggy ink cap

Field mushroom

Oyster mushroom

Death-cap

FACTS: Poisonous fungi

- **Fly agaric**
Fly agaric makes the poison muscarine which causes stomach pains and convulsions, and can occasionally kill. Fly agaric was once taken in small doses for its hallucinatory effect.

- **Death-cap**
The death-cap and destroying angel toadstools look quite like harmless mushrooms — but they are deadly. Death-cap contains the poisons amanitine and phalloidine which can kill a human within six hours of eating it, due to kidney and liver failure.

- **False morel**
False morel makes the poison gyromitrin which can create terrible stomach pains.

▶ Fly agaric announces its deadly poison with its bright colour. Eating even small amounts can completely knock you out.

Algae

A KIND OF ALGAE was among the first living things to appear on Earth some 3 billion years ago. There are now many different kinds of algae, and although some are tiny, they are very important. They grow almost everywhere there is water, from the oceans to damp walls. Algae in the oceans not only provide food for creatures such as whales, but maintain the levels of oxygen in the air – and without this we could not breathe. Algae can draw energy from sunlight like most plants, but they have neither leaves, stems, roots or flowers. Indeed, many scientists don't put algae in the plant kingdom at all but in their own kingdom called *Protoctista*.

FACTS: About lichens

◀ Lichens grow on bare rock, and can often be seen on stone walls and old stone buildings. But they are very sensitive to any pollution in the air — especially sulphur dioxide from coal-fired power stations — and will not grow where the air is dirty.

▼ Lichens grow in three kinds of shapes. Crusty or 'crustose' lichens grow in discs on stones and walls. Leafy or 'foliose' lichens grow on the ground or on trees, and their edges curl up like leaves. Shrubby or 'fruticose' lichens look like tiny bushes.

Crustose lichen

- **Algae and fungi**
  Lichens look like plants. But they are actually a remarkable partnership between algae and fungi. The algae are tiny green balls, and use sunlight to make food for the fungi. The fungi create a protective blanket above and below and act as a water store.

- **Reindeer food**
  The algae–fungi partnership enables lichens to live on bare rock faces and very harsh places such as the Antarctic and on mountaintops. If things get too dry or cold, they simply go into suspended animation, ready for the good times to begin again. Some lichens provide the only food for reindeer in the Arctic.

FACTS: About seaweed

- **Large algae**
  Seaweeds are very large algae that grow on seashores, or get washed up on beaches. They are usually brown, red or green in colour. They tend to grow in the shallows because they need sunlight.

- **Brown and red**
  Brown algae such as kelp grow 15-20m down. Fern-like red algae grow at a depth of 30-60m.

- **Holding on**
  Seaweeds have a 'holdfast', which looks like a mass of roots, but is just the seaweed's suckers for holding on to rocks despite crashing waves. They actually rely on the water to support them.

- **Natural floats**
  Some seaweeds have air-filled bladders to help them float near the surface.

- **Useful weeds**
  In many places, seaweed is gathered from the seashore to put on the land as fertilizer. It is also a valuable source of iodine and some antibiotics. 'Alginates' from seaweeds help set ice-cream.

Seaweed helps oxygenate the water, and provides grazing for many sea creatures

- **Sea food**
  Seaweed may not look appetizing, but it is popular in Chinese and Japanese cooking. The red seaweed Porphyra is used in Wales to make a kind of pudding called 'laver-bread'

FACTS: About algae

- **Plankton**
  In the oceans, the most important plants are 'phytoplankton' — tiny organisms that float in the surface waters of the oceans and grow in huge numbers. These are food for a wide range of sea creatures.

- **Algal bloom**
  Sometimes algae grow in such huge numbers that they choke other life. These 'algal blooms' can sometimes be caused in rivers by fertilizer pollution from farms.

▶ Most seaweeds stay submerged all the time, but many have to cope with the tides — and long periods when they are left high and dry out of water. Some can survive almost a day in baking sunshine, drying up, then returning to life when the tide comes in and refreshes them again. In fact, seaweeds are banded in the tide zone according to how long they can live out of water.

Plants for food

PLANTS PROVIDE the 'staple' (basic or essential) food for most people around the world, and an area one and a half times the size of the USA is used for growing crops. Over 12,000 species of plant have been used for food at one time or other, but only about 150 or so are regularly grown as crops, including cereals such as wheat, rice and maize, fruit such as oranges and bananas, root vegetables such as potatoes and yams, green vegetables such as cabbage and kale, and pulses such as soya beans and lentils. Some of these were first cultivated over 10,000 years ago.

FACTS: Fruit and vegetables

- **Citrus fruits**
  Oranges, lemons, grapefruits, tangerines and limes are citrus fruits and are grown in huge quantities in places with Mediterranean climates. The fruits are picked in winter and often made into juice.

- **Fruit farms**
  Apples are grown in orchards, oranges are grown in groves and bananas on plantations.

- **Potato blight**
  Potatoes come originally from America, but they became the staple for poor Irish farmers in the 19th century. When the potato crop was ruined by a disease called 'blight' in the 1840s, millions of Irish people starved.

▶ *Bananas are the major export of many countries in Central America, such as El Salvador and Honduras. They are picked while still green and semi-frozen for export by sea.*

Millet is grown in dry places such as Africa and is ground to make flour

Sunflower seeds are crushed to produce oil

▶ *These are just some of the plants grown for food. Many, including sunflowers, corn (maize) and olives are made into oil. The cereals can be ground to make flour, but rice is usually cooked as whole grains, while maize, millet and sorghum (as well as oats) are typically made into a kind of porridge. Maize comes in two kinds. One gives the large head with lots of grains, known as sweetcorn or corn on the cob. Smaller-grained, smaller-headed maize is used for corn oil or cornflour.*

Olives grow on trees in Mediterranean areas. They are eaten whole or pressed to make oil

Sorghum is a cereal grown in places such as Egypt and China

Wheat

Maize

Rice

▲ Sugar cane is a tall plant grown in warm places such as the Caribbean. To make sugar, the cane is crushed to make a sugary liquid which is then boiled and condensed until crystals form. These crystals are white sugar which may then be further refined to make icing sugar and castor sugar, or even compressed to make sugar lumps.

Barley is grown in temperate regions. It is used for food as well as for making alcoholic drinks

FACTS: About cereals

• **What are cereals?**
Cereals are crops such as wheat, maize, rice, oats, rye and barley. They are all grasses and we eat the seeds or grain, leaving the stalks and leaves to rot into animal food called silage.

• **Wheat**
Wheat provides the basic food for over one in three people in the world. Wheat grain is ground to make flour which is then used to make things such as bread and pasta.

• **Rice**
Widely grown in southern Asia, rice is the staple food for half the world's population. In China alone, 190 million tonnes are grown every year. There are over 14,000 types, including many long-grained rices such as Basmati rice used with Indian curries, medium-grained rices used for Italian risotto, and short-grained rice used for puddings. Brown rice is white rice with the husk on.

• **Paddy fields**
Rice is the only cereal crop grown in water — in flooded fields called 'paddies'. Most of the work in producing it is done by hand. There are typically three crops a year.

▶ Before processing, rice grains are enclosed in tough husks. Removing this outer layer makes brown rice; refining the grains even further makes white rice.

Herbs and spices

HERBS AND SPICES HAVE BEEN used to flavour food and to make medicines since prehistoric times. Herbs are small flowering plants, and there are hundreds of different kinds, each with its own special properties. Usually it is the leaves that are valued, but it can be the flowers or the stem. Some, such as basil and oregano, are edible, and used in small quantities to flavour food. Others, like feverfew, are valued more for their medicinal qualities. Spices are strongly flavoured seeds, roots and bark that are usually ground into powder to add to food as it is cooked.

FACTS: About tea and coffee

- **Tea**
  Tea is the dried leaves of a small camellia bush that grows on hillsides in subtropical areas, especially in India and Sri Lanka, Japan and China. The best tea grows slowly at high altitudes (up to 2,000m in places).

- **Black tea and green tea**
  There are two main kinds of tea: green tea and black tea. Green tea is picked and dried quickly, giving a mild flavour. Green tea is popular in China. Black tea is only partly dried before it is crushed in rolling machines, giving a much stronger flavour. Black tea is preferred in Europe.

- **Coffee**
  Coffee is made from the ground and roasted beans of the coffee bush. The beans are collected and soaked, then the husks are removed and the beans are dried, sorted and roasted. The longer the roast, the stronger and darker the coffee.

- **Instant coffee**
  Coffee can be made into instant coffee powder by boiling coffee dry, or into instant coffee granules by plunging ground beans into liquid gas to freeze-dry them.

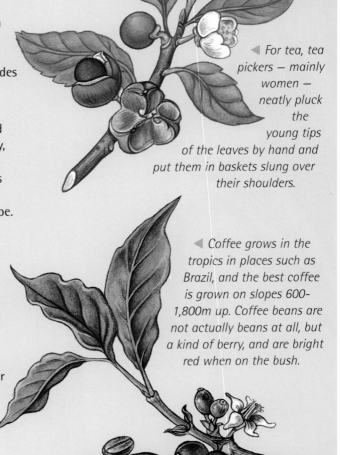

◀ For tea, tea pickers — mainly women — neatly pluck the young tips of the leaves by hand and put them in baskets slung over their shoulders.

◀ Coffee grows in the tropics in places such as Brazil, and the best coffee is grown on slopes 600-1,800m up. Coffee beans are not actually beans at all, but a kind of berry, and are bright red when on the bush.

FACTS: About herbs

- **Herbal drugs**

  Many of today's medicines came originally from plants, including aspirin (from willow trees), morphine (from the seeds of the opium poppy) and quinine (from the bark of the cinchona tree of South America). An extract of the rosy periwinkle, called vincristine, is one of the drugs used against leukaemia, childhood cancer.

- **Herb facts**

  Egyptian pyramid builders ate garlic because they thought it would give them strength. Rosemary gets its name from the Latin *ros marinus* which means sea dew. Bay leaves were used to crown poets and heroes in Ancient Rome. The Ancient Greeks called basil 'King of Herbs'. The Latin name for sage is Salvia, which means healthy, and sage is thought to have healing qualities. Mint and the spice cinnamon keep moths away from clothes. Oregano is used as a dye as well as a food flavour.

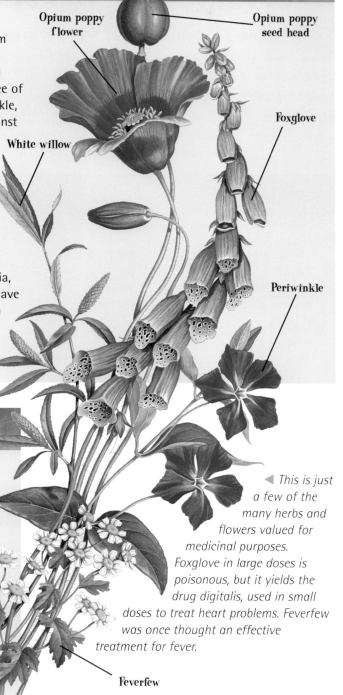

Opium poppy flower

Opium poppy seed head

Foxglove

White willow

Periwinkle

FACTS: About spices

- **Spice facts**

  It takes 400,000 hand-picked crocus flower heads to make 1kg of saffron. Ginger is the root of a tall grass-like plant which is harvested after flowering. Even though it is a hot spice, chilli can cool you down because it makes you sweat. Cinnamon comes from the bark of a tree. Nutmeg is the seed of a tree. Star anise takes 15 years to grow.

- **Spice islands**

  Many spices come from the Moluccas in Indonesia, which were once known as the Spice Islands.

◀ This is just a few of the many herbs and flowers valued for medicinal purposes. Foxglove in large doses is poisonous, but it yields the drug digitalis, used in small doses to treat heart problems. Feverfew was once thought an effective treatment for fever.

Feverfew

Tropical plants

 The tropics are warm nearly all the time, and in the rainforests there is abundant moisture. The combination creates almost ideal conditions for plant growth, and tropical forests are not only lush but contain an astonishing variety of plants – including some of the world's most spectacular and strange. The rainforests are the world's richest plant habitats, containing over 40 per cent of the world's plant species. Noone knows exactly how many different plants there are. But botanists counted over 180 species of tree alone in one hectare of the Malaysian forest.

FACTS: Coping with drought

- **Deep roots**
  When there is no water on the surface, plants can often find moisture deep underground by growing long roots. Mesquite roots often grow as deep as 10m, and may be as long as 50m.

- **Tough leaves**
  In moist places, plants lose water by evaporation from their leaves. So desert plants usually have tough, waxy leaves that cut moisture loss to a minimum – and have as few leaves as possible.

▲ The baobab of Africa and Australia survives in dry places by retaining moisture in its barrel-shaped trunk, which can be up to 9m thick.

- **Cacti**
  Cacti live in American deserts. They have no leaves and a thick skin, so water loss is cut to a minimum. Their fat stems can hold huge amounts of water, which is why they are called succulents.

- **Prickly plants**
  Lush vegetation is so rare in deserts that animals eat anything. So cacti, prickly pears and thorn bushes grow prickles to protect themselves.

◀ Cacti have to pollinate, just like every other flowering plant and so every few years they produce big colourful blooms in order to attract insects quickly.

FACTS: About tropical water plants

- **Amazon lily**
  The world's biggest water plant is the Amazon water lily of South America. Its massive floating leaves grow up to 2m across, and can sometimes support the weight of a child.

- **Water hyacinth**
  The water hyacinth is the world's fastest growing water plant — so fast growing that it is thought of as a pest, especially since it chokes waterways and encourages mosquitoes.

Rafflesia has no stem - just a huge flower which sits on the ground

◀ The rafflesia of southeast Asia is the world's biggest flower. A single bloom can be 1m across and weigh up to 7kg. It is said to smell like rotting meat — perhaps to attract the flies it needs to help it pollinate.

Key facts: Plants

Parts of a flower

There are two kinds of flowering plants: monocotyledons and dicotyledons. Monocotyledons have one leaf sprout, e.g. grasses, cereals, tulips and daffodils. Dicotyledons have two leaf sprouts, e.g. most deciduous trees, vegetables and fruits. Pollen is made in the 'anthers' on top of the stamens, the male parts of the flower. The female part, or pistil, is topped by a sticky 'stigma', which traps the pollen. A long tube or 'style' takes it down to the ovary where it meets the eggs to create the seeds.

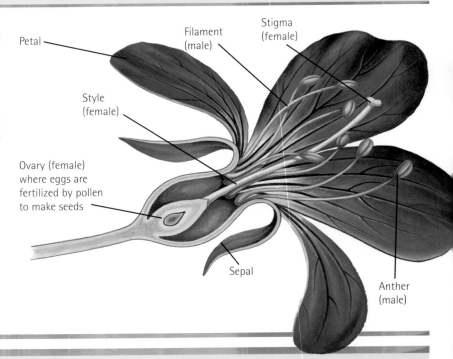

Petal

Filament (male)

Stigma (female)

Style (female)

Ovary (female) where eggs are fertilized by pollen to make seeds

Sepal

Anther (male)

Plant evolution

- Fossils show that the first plants appeared on Earth more than 1 billion years ago. They lived in the ocean and probably looked like small lumps of green slime.
- Gradually these earliest plants developed into larger algae, or seaweeds.
- About 400 million years ago, small moss-like plants spread slowly on to the rocky, empty land.
- By 300 million years ago, ferns grew as big as trees, forming steamy, swampy prehistoric forests.
- Some 200 million years ago, forests of conifer trees spread across the land, as the first dinosaurs roamed among them.
- Flowering plants appeared about 130 million years ago, bringing bright colours to the landscape.

The plant kingdom

Scientific group name	Ordinary name	Approx. number of different species
Algae	Seaweeds	6,000
Bryophytes	Mosses	10,000
	Liverworts	14,000
Pteridophytes	Ferns	12,000
	Horsetails	30
	Clubmosses	400
Gymnosperms	Conifers	600
Angiosperms	Flowering plants	250,000 +

Fungi

1. Rusts and mildews
2. Moulds
3. Sac fungi
4. Club fungi
5. Imperfect fungi
6. Slime moulds

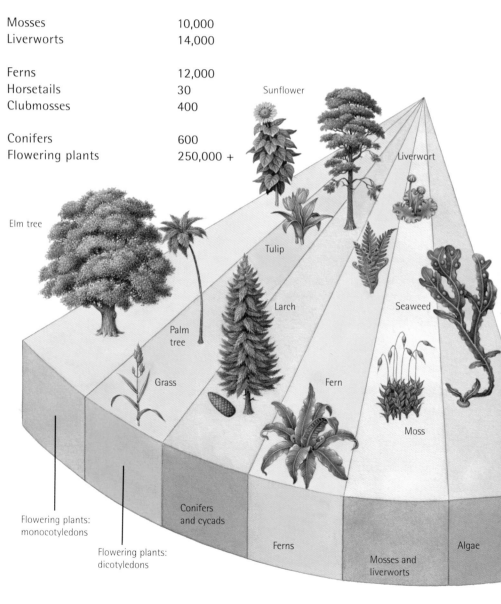

Elm tree

Sunflower

Liverwort

Tulip

Palm tree

Larch

Seaweed

Grass

Fern

Moss

Flowering plants: monocotyledons

Flowering plants: dicotyledons

Conifers and cycads

Ferns

Mosses and liverworts

Algae

Key facts: Plants

Plant records

- **The smallest plant**
  The smallest plant is the duckweed wolffia arrhiza, which has fronds less than 1mm across.
- **The biggest plant**
  The biggest plant is the giant sequioa tree called General Sherman in California which is 83m tall and 25m round the trunk.
- **The oldest living thing**
  The oldest living thing is a lichen in Antarctica thought to be over 10,000 years old.
- **Tallest tree ever measured**
  A eucalyptus in Victoria, Australia, was 143m tall.

- **The biggest flower**
  The biggest flower is the rafflesia of Indonesia, which has blooms more than 90cm across.
- **The biggest water plant**
  The biggest water plant is the Amazon water lily, which has leaves more than 2m across.
- **The biggest leaves**
  The biggest leaves belong to the raffia palm, which can grow up to 20m long.
- **The deepest roots**
  The deepest roots belong to a fig tree growing in South Africa, which has roots down more than 120m.
- **The biggest seed**
  The biggest seed is the coco de mer coconut, which weighs up to 20kg.
- **The fastest growing plant**
  The fastest growing plant is the bamboo, which can grow up to 91cm in a single day.

Some major food crops

CEREALS	SUGAR	VEGETABLES	NON-FOOD PLANTS
Wheat	Sugarcane	Tomatoes	Trees for
Rice	Sugarbeet	Squash	timber and
Corn			paper
Barley	FRUITS AND	LEAVES	Cotton
Oats	NUTS	Lettuce	Tobacco
Rye	Apples	Cabbage	Rubber
	Oranges		Jute
ROOT CROPS	Bananas	HERBS AND	Coir
Potatoes	Grapes	SPICES	Flax
Yams	Mangoes	Parsley	Sisal
Cassava	Melons	Basil	Kapok
Manioc	Blueberries	Chilli	Hops
	Hazelnuts	Chocolate	
	Peanuts		

Plants also provide 80% of all our fuels. The main fossil fuels are coal, oil and natural gas.

Plant environments

Temperate woodlands
Deciduous
- trees such as beech, birch, hickory, maple, oak, poplar and walnut
- shrubs such as bramble, hawthorn and honeysuckle
- woodland flowers such as bluebell, primrose, foxglove, willowherb and anenome

Coniferous
- trees such as redwood, giant sequoia, Douglas fir, cedar and pine
- small trees such as rowan and hazel
- fern
- bilberry

Grasslands
- grasses such as tussock, marram, meadow and rye
- trees and shrubs such as acacia, thorn, baobab and rokerboom

- flowers such as vetches, trefoils, orchids, blazing star, worts and coneflowers

Tropical forests
- trees such as mahogany, teak, banyan and palm
- lichen
- vine and liana
- epiphytes such as orchid, fern, tree fern and bromeliad
- carnivorous plants such as Venus fly traps and pitcher plants

Lakes and rivers
- reed, rush and papyrus
- sedge
- worts such as bladderwort and fanwort
- water crowfoot
- waterlily and iris
- water hyacinth

Deserts
- cactus
- creosote bush, thorn tree, quiver tree, Joshua tree, sagebrush, yucca and prickly pear
- window plants and pebble plant
- palm tree
- evening primrose

High mountains
- rowan and dwarf willow, crowberry and bilberry
- wild flowers such as alpine bluebell, mountain aven, gentian, edelweiss, snowbell, saxifrage and saussurea
- grass and moss

Quiz: Plants

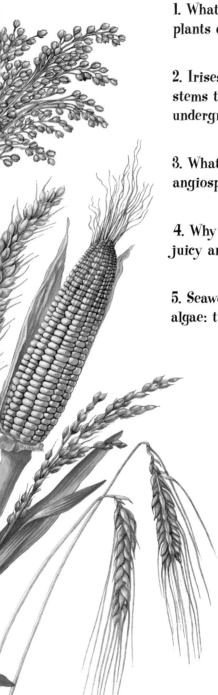

1. What are the biggest plants on Earth?

2. Irises grow from thick stems that grow sideways underground: true or false?

3. What kind of plant is an angiosperm?

4. Why are fruits often juicy and sweet?

5. Seaweeds are a kind of algae: true or false?

6. Which part of a plant draws up water from the ground?

7. Some plants take their food from other plants, rather than from the earth: true or false?

8. Some ferns can grow up to 25m tall: true or false?

9. Plants need to absorb something through their leaves in order to turn carbon dioxide from the air and hydrogen from water into food. What do they need to absorb?

10. The giant sequoia tree in California is the world's biggest living thing. It is 154m tall: true or false?

11. What is the seed of the oak tree called?

12. The tubes that carry water up a plant's stem are called xylophones: true or false?

13. The oldest surviving species of tree comes from China and first appeared more than 160 million years ago. What is the tree called?

14. Potatoes originally came from Ireland: true or false?

15. What part of the sunflower plant is sunflower oil made from?

16. It takes 182,000 hand-picked crocus flower heads to make 450g of saffron (a spice used to flavour rice): true or false?

17. What important food crop is grown in water-filled fields in southern Asia?

18. Lichen growing in Antarctica may be the world's oldest living thing. It is thought to be more than 10,000 years old: true or false?

19. The leaves of the Amazon water lily are nearly 2m across: true or false?

20. Do pine trees lose their leaves in winter?

Answers:

1. Trees
2. True
3. A flowering plant
4. So that animals are tempted to eat them and spread the seeds in their droppings
5. True
6. The roots
7. True
8. True
9. Sunlight
10. False - it is 83m tall
11. Acorn
12. False - they are called xylem
13. The maidenhair tree
14. False - they came from South America
15. The seeds of the sunflower
16. True
17. Rice
18. True
19. True
20. No

THE UNIVERSE

Planet Earth

THIRD PLANET OUT FROM THE SUN, our Earth looks from a distance like a great round blue jewel hanging in the darkness of space. It is blue because three-quarters of its rocky surface is drowned under blue ocean waters which shimmer in the light of the Sun. No other planet has this much water on its surface. Here and there, its rocky surface pokes up above the water to form half a dozen large continents and thousands of smaller islands. The very ends of the world are glistening white – the polar ice caps.

FACTS: Earth measurements

- **The size of the Earth**
  Modern measurements show the distance round the Earth is 40,024km at the equator. The Earth's diameter at the equator is 12,758km — slightly larger than its diameter pole to pole, by 43km.

- **The weight of the Earth**
  The Earth weighs 6,000 trillion trillion tonnes.

- **The angle of the Earth**
  The Earth tilts over at an angle of 23.45°.

▼ *Satellites have allowed the Earth to be measured more accurately than ever before. Satellites can detect movements of the continents of just a few millimetres or small variations in the height of the sea's surface.*

▲ *The Earth looks round, but it is not a perfect sphere. Because it spins faster at the equator than the poles, it is actually shaped more like a tangerine, bulging slightly at the equator and flattened at the poles. So scientists used to describe its shape as an oblate spheroid (flattened ball). Now satellite measurements have detected other slight irregularities, so they call it a geoid, which simply means Earth-shaped.*

FACTS: Inside the Earth

- **Probing the Earth**
  Scientists have worked out what the Earth's interior is like from vibrations from earthquakes and underground explosions.

- **Crust**
  The Earth has a thin shell of solid rock called the crust, which varies from 6–11km under the oceans to 30–70km under the continents.

- **Mantle**
  Beneath the crust is a layer almost 3,000km deep, called the mantle. It is so hot here that the rock often flows like sticky treacle — only very, very slowly.

- **Core**
  Below the mantle is a core of metal, mostly iron and nickel.

- **Outer core**
  The outer portion of the core is so ferociously hot that the metal is always molten.

- **Inner core**
  The Earth's inner core is even hotter — up to 7,000°C — but the metal here is solid because pressures here are so great that metal simply cannot melt.

Inner core   Outer core   Mantle   Crust

▲ The Earth has several different layers because the materials it is made of have separated out over billions of years. Dense metals such as iron sank to the centre to form the core, while lighter rock-forming materials floated to the top to form the crust.

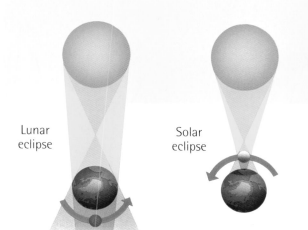

Lunar eclipse

Solar eclipse

◀ Every now and then, the Earth and Moon get in between each other and the Sun. This is called an eclipse because the planet in between 'eclipses,' or blocks out, the Sun. A lunar eclipse is when the Moon goes round behind the Earth into its shadow. A solar eclipse is when the Moon comes in between the Sun and the Earth, casting a shadow a few kilometres wide on the Earth.

The Moon

Earthrise on the Moon

THE MOON IS THE BIGGEST, BRIGHTEST object in the night sky. It seems to shine almost like a pale sun. But it does not give out any light itself. It is just a big, cold ball of rock. It shines only because it reflects sunlight. The Moon is the Earth's companion in space, and circles round it continuously, just as the Earth circles the Sun. The Moon is about a quarter of the Earth's size and was probably formed shortly after the Earth, perhaps from hot splashes flung out as a small planet collided with the Earth.

FACTS: About the Moon

- **Pitted surface**
  The Moon's surface is pitted with craters — dents created by the impact of huge rocks early in its history.

- **Seas on the Moon**
  All over the Moon's surface are dark patches which people once believed were seas. In fact, they are not seas at all, but vast plains formed by lava flowing from volcanoes that erupted early in the Moon's history.

- **'Moonths'**
  The word month comes from the Moon, and the time it takes to go once round the Earth. It takes the Moon 27.3 days to circle the Earth, but it actually takes 29.53 days from one full moon to the next, because the Earth moves as well, and the Moon falls a little behind. This 29.53 days cycle is called a lunar month. However, the length of our calendar months was decided a few centuries ago by the Pope.

- **Watery Moon**
  In 1998, X-ray cameras on an American space probe revealed that there are huge quantities of water on the Moon, in the form of ice under the Moon's surface.

The moon's rocky mantle is cool and solid, unlike the Earth's mantle

The Moon's outer core is probably solid metal

The Moon has a small inner core of molten metal

▲ The Moon's surface is very dead compared with the Earth's. It has no atmosphere. The surface is just fine white dust, pitted with craters. Also, its rocky interior is cool, not hot like the Earth's, and the volcanic activity which constantly changes the Earth's surface has long since died out on the Moon.

FACTS: On the Moon

▲ *The Moon is the only world beyond ours that people have visited. When Neil Armstrong set foot on it on 21 July 1969, he said famously, 'That's one small step for a man, one giant leap for mankind'.*

- **Men on the Moon**
  The first men to land on the Moon were Neil Armstrong and Buzz Aldrin — in July 1969. The most recent was Eugene Cernan in December 1972.

- **High jumping**
  The Moon's gravity is only a sixth of the Earth's, so everything is very light. Moon astronauts can jump easily – even in heavy space suits.

- **Footprints forever**
  Because there is no air, the sky on the Moon is inky black even in daytime, and there is no wind to ruffle the dust. So the footprints left by the first men on the Moon will be there forever.

- **Day and night**
  Each day on the Moon lasts 360 hours, and the temperature reaches 127°C — but the night is just as long and temperatures plunge to -162°C.

The phases of the Moon

Only the part of the Moon lit by the Sun is bright enough for us to see. But as it circles the Earth, the Sun shines on the Moon from changing angles, and we see more or less of the moon at different times — and so the Moon appears to change shape over the course of a month as it circles the Earth. These changes are called phases.

▼ *During the first half of the month, the Moon grows from a crescent-shaped new Moon, to a half Moon, to a full Moon. This is called waxing. In the second half, it gets smaller or 'wanes' through a half Moon back to a crescent-shaped old Moon — curving the opposite way from the new Moon.*

The Sun

THE SUN IS OUR LOCAL STAR, a vast fiery spinning ball of hot gases – three quarters hydrogen and a quarter helium. It is well over a million times as big as the Earth. The gigantic mass of the Sun creates immense pressures in its core. Such huge pressures fuse hydrogen atoms together in a continual nuclear reaction that boosts temperatures to 15 billion°C. All this heat turns the outer surface of the sun into a raging inferno that burns so brightly that it completely floodlights the Earth, over 1.5 million kilometres away.

FACTS: Inside the sun

- **A bomb in the heart**
  Pressures in the Sun's core are 2,000 billion times the pressure of the Earth's atmosphere. These fuse so many hydrogen atoms together that it is as if 100 billion nuclear bombs were going off each second.

- **All down to Einstein**
  We owe our understanding of how the Sun produces heat and light to the famous scientist Albert Einstein (1897–1955), who showed how mass can be changed into energy.

- **Surface layers**
  The visible surface layer of the Sun is the photosphere. Above this lies the chromosphere and the corona.

- **Hot surface**
  Temperatures at the surface of the Sun are a phenomenal 6,000°C, enough to melt almost anything. Each square centimetre burns with the brightness of 250,000 candles.

- **The Sun's age**
  The Sun probably formed about 5 billion years ago, just a little before the Earth, which formed from the debris left over. It will burn out in about 5 billion years time.

- **The solar wind**
  Streaming out from the Sun every second are a million tonnes of electrically charged particles. Earth is protected from this lethal stream, called the solar wind, by its magnetic field.

- **SOHO**
  The SOHO space observatory sits in space between Earth and Sun and monitors the Sun continually.

◄ *The Sun's energy is generated by nuclear reactions in its core and makes its way to the surface over millions of years.*

DATA: The Sun

- **DIAMETER**
  The Sun is a medium-sized star 1,392,000km across – 10 times the diameter of the Earth.

- **MASS**
  The Sun weighs 2,000 trillion trillion tonnes – over 300,000 times the weight of the Earth.

- **ENERGY CONSUMPTION**
  The Sun burns up 4 million tonnes of hydrogen fuel every second.

- **ENERGY PRODUCTION**
  The Sun's energy production each second could keep the USA supplied with electricity for 50 million years.

- **CORONAL TEMPERATURE**
  The temperature of the Sun's outer ring or corona is 1.5 million°C.

▲ *Every now and then, the Moon swings between the Sun and the Earth, blocking out the Sun and creating a shadow a few hundred kilometres wide on the Earth. This is called a solar eclipse. Sometimes, the Sun glints through a valley on the Moon's surface, as in this picture, creating an effect like a jewel on a ring.*

▶ *The heat from the Sun's core erupts on the surface in patches called granules. Here and there, giant flame-like tongues of hot hydrogen, called solar prominences, loop 100,000km out into space. Every now and then, too, huge five-minute eruptions of energy called solar flares burst from the surface. In places, there are dark blotches on the Sun's surface, called sunspots, over 50 times the size of Africa. They are dark because they are slightly less hot than the rest of the surface. The number of spots seems to peak every 11 years, and some scientists believe these peaks are linked to spells of stormier weather on Earth.*

Inner planets

Mercury

THE INNER PLANETS are the four planets in the solar system that are nearest the Sun. Nearest the Sun is little Mercury, then comes Mars, Earth and Venus. All four are made of rock, unlike the big planets further out, which are made mainly of gas. Because they are made of rock, they have a hard surface which a spaceship could land on, and they are sometimes called terrestrial (earth-like) planets. They all have an atmosphere of gas above the rocky surface – although Mercury's is very thin – but each is very different.

FACTS: About Mercury

◀ Mercury's atmosphere of sodium is so thin that there is nothing to stop meteors smashing into its surface — and nothing to smooth out any dents. So its surface is more deeply pitted with the scars of meteor impacts than the Moon's. All you'd see on a voyage across the surface would be vast empty basins, cliffs and endless views of yellow dust.

- **Hot and cold**
  Temperatures on Mercury veer from one extreme to the other because its atmosphere is too thin to provide any insulation. In the day, temperatures soar to 430°C, but at night they plunge to -180°C.

- **Mercury's brief year**
  Mercury is so near the Sun that its orbit is very short. It gets round in just 88 days, compared with 365 days for the Earth. On the other hand, it takes a long time to turn round — 58.6 days. So its day lasts 58.6 Earth days.

- **Burning cold**
  Mercury has small ice caps at each pole — but the ice is made from acid, not water.

DATA: The inner planets

MERCURY
- Mercury is 45.9 million km from the Sun at its closest and 69.7 million km at its furthest.
- Mercury's diameter is 4,878km and its mass is barely a twentieth of the Earth's.

VENUS
- Venus is 107.4 million km from the Sun at its closest and 109 million km at its furthest.
- Venus's diameter is 12,102km and its mass is about four-fifths that of the Earth's.

MARS
- Mars is 227.9 million km from the Sun.
- Mars's diameter is 6,786km and its mass is just over a tenth of the Earth's.

FACTS: About Venus

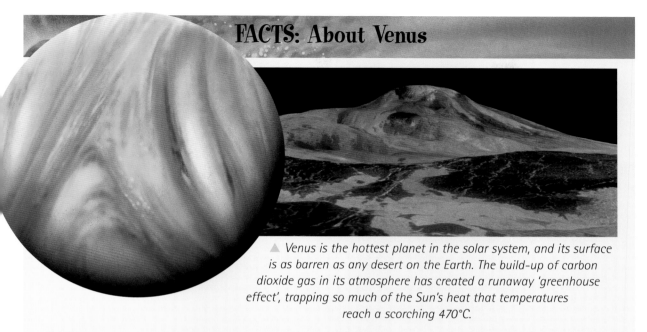

▲ Venus is the hottest planet in the solar system, and its surface is as barren as any desert on the Earth. The build-up of carbon dioxide gas in its atmosphere has created a runaway 'greenhouse effect', trapping so much of the Sun's heat that temperatures reach a scorching 470°C.

- **Evening star**
  Venus reflects sunlight so well off its thick atmosphere that it shines like a star. But because it is quite close to the Sun, we can see it only in the evening just after the sun has gone down, which is why it is sometimes called the evening star. We can also see it just before sunrise.

- **Thick air**
  Venus's atmosphere would be deadly to humans. It is very deep and thick, so pressure on the surface is enormous. It is also made mainly of poisonous carbon dioxide and filled with clouds of sulphuric acid gas belched out by the volcanoes on its surface.

FACTS: About Mars

- **High and deep**
  Mars has the biggest volcano in the solar system, called Olympus Mons, 15km high, three times higher than Mt Everest. It also has a canyon called Valles Marineris which is 4,000km long and four times as deep as the Grand Canyon.

- **The red planet**
  None of the space missions to Mars so far has found even the remotest trace of life. But, in 1996, NASA scientists found what they thought might be the fossil of a microscopic organism in a rock from Mars in the Arctic. So the search is on.

▶ Mars is sometimes called the red planet because it is rusty red. The surface contains a high proportion of iron dust, and this has been oxidized (rusted) in its carbon dioxide-rich atmosphere. It has small ice caps.

Giant planets

Saturn

OUT BEYOND MARS THERE are two planets far bigger than any others in the solar system. Jupiter and Saturn, the fifth and sixth planets out from the Sun, are gigantic. Jupiter is twice as heavy as all the other planets put together and 1,300 times as big as the Earth. Saturn is not that much smaller. Unlike the inner planets, though, they are both made mostly of gas, and only their very core is rocky. This doesn't mean they are vast cloud balls. The huge pressure of gravity means the gas is squeezed until it becomes liquid or even solid.

FACTS: About Jupiter

◄ *Jupiter's surface is covered in a thin layer of swirling clouds of ammonia, indicating powerful storms. One storm called the Great Red Spot is 40,000km across and has lasted at least 330 years.*

• **Mighty magnet**
Jupiter's bulk and its fast spin churn up the metal insides of the planet so much that the planet becomes a giant dynamo creating a magnetic field ten times as strong as the Earth's.

• **Many moons**
Jupiter has 16 moons. There are four big ones discovered by Galileo as long ago as 1610, which is why they are called the Galilean moons. Then there are 12 smaller ones.

Great Red Spot

Galilean moon

▼ *The power of Jupiter's gravity drags volcanoes of sulphur from the surface of its moon Io.*

• **Fast spinner**
Jupiter spins faster than any other planet. Despite its vast size, it turns right round in just 9.8 hours, so the surface is moving at 45,000kmh!

• **Hydrogen deeps**
Jupiter is made mostly of hydrogen and helium gas, but this is squeezed so hard by the planet's gravity that it turns to liquid. Beneath Jupiter's thin atmosphere of ammonia, there is an ocean of liquid hydrogen 25,000km deep.

FACTS: About Saturn

 Saturn is the most beautiful of all the planets, with its pale butterscotch surface of ammonia gases and its huge halo of rings.

- **Saturn's rings**
  Saturn's rings are countless billions of tiny chips of ice and dust, few bigger than a refrigerator and most smaller than an ice cube. The rings are thin — no more than 50m deep — yet stretch over 74,000km out into space.

▼ Saturn's rings have definite bands, named with the letters A to G.

- **Light planet**
  Saturn may be big, but it is surprisingly light, weighing 600 billion trillion tonnes. If you had a large enough bath, it would float.

- **Most moons**
  Saturn has more moons than any other planet — at least 19. Iapetus is black on one side and white on the other. Enceladus is covered in shimmering balls of ice. Tethys was once almost split in half by a giant meteor which left a giant crater. Titan is the only moon with an atmosphere.

- **Windy planet**
  The winds on the surface of Saturn are faster than those on Jupiter, roaring around at 1,800kmh.

 # DATA: About the giant planets

JUPITER
- Jupiter is 740.9 million km from the Sun at its closest and 815.7 million km at its furthest.
- Jupiter's diameter is 142,984km and its mass is 318 times that of the Earth's.
- It takes 11.86 years to orbit the Sun.
- Its surface temperature is -150°C.

SATURN
- Saturn is 1,347 million km from the Sun at its closest and 1,507 million km at its furthest.
- Saturn's diameter is 120,536km and its mass is over 95 times that of the Earth's.
- It takes 29.46 years to orbit the Sun.
- Its surface temperature is -180°C.

Outer planets

OUT BEYOND SATURN are the seventh, eight and ninth planets of the solar system, Uranus, Neptune and Pluto, along with Pluto's companion Charon. Unlike the other planets, these were unknown to ancient astronomers. They are so far away and so faint that Uranus was discovered only in 1781, Neptune in 1846, Pluto in 1930 and Charon as recently as 1978. Uranus and Neptune are giant gas planets like Saturn and Jupiter. Pluto and Charon are rocky planets and may have been asteroids trapped by the Sun's gravity in the outer reaches of the solar system.

Neptune

FACTS: About Uranus

- **Rollover planet**
  Unlike any of the other planets, Uranus does not spin at a slight angle. Instead it is tilted right over, and rolls around the Sun like a giant bowling ball. In summer, the Sun does not set for 20 years.

- **Blue planet**
  Uranus has an atmosphere of hydrogen and helium, but beneath that are oceans of liquid methane, and it is this that gives the planet its beautiful blue-green colour.

◀ Uranus is so far from the Sun that temperatures drop to -210°C. Winds whistle through its atmosphere at 2,000kmh, whipping up huge waves in the icy oceans of methane below.

FACTS: About Neptune

◀ Neptune has its own thin set of rings, like Saturn's.

- **Blue planet**
  Like Uranus, Neptune has a thin atmosphere of hydrogen and helium, but is mostly deep oceans of liquid methane. The methane makes Neptune a beautiful cobalt blue.

- **Long year**
  Neptune is so far from the Sun — over 4 billion km — that its orbit takes 164.79 years.

- **Discovering Neptune**
  Neptune's moon Triton is the only moon to orbit backwards. It is the coldest place in the solar system (-236°C) and looks like a green melon with pink ice cream on the ends — ice caps of frozen nitrogen. Its volcanoes erupt ice.

DATA: The outer planets

URANUS
- Uranus is 2,735 million km from the Sun at its closest and 3,004 million km at its furthest.
- Uranus's diameter is 51,118km and its mass is over 14 times that of the Earth's.

NEPTUNE
- Neptune is 4,456 million km from the Sun at its closest and 4,537 million km at its furthest.

- Neptune's diameter is 49,528km and its mass is over 17 times that of the Earth's.

PLUTO
- Pluto is 4,730 million km from the Sun at its closest and 7,375 million km at its furthest.
- Pluto's diameter is 2,840km and its mass is just a fiftieth of the Earth's.

- **Discovering Neptune**
  Neptune was discovered because in the 1840s two young mathematicians, John Couch Adams in England and Urbain le Verrier in France, predicted where it should be from the way its gravity made a slight difference to Uranus's orbit. The planet was actually spotted by John Galle from the Berlin observatory on 23 September 1846.

▼ *This is a view of Neptune and its moon Triton taken by the Voyager space mission which reached the planet in 1989.*

FACTS: About Pluto

▶ *Pluto and Charon are so far away from the Sun that the Sun looks little bigger in their sky than a star, and shines as palely as the Moon on the Earth. So surface temperatures plunge to -220°C.*

- **Pluto**
  Pluto is very, very small, which is why it took so long to spot. Indeed some people say it should not be called a planet at all. It is five times smaller than the Earth — just 2.284km across — and 500 times lighter.

- **Charon**
  Pluto is only twice as big as its companion moon Charon. So they circle round each other locked in space like a pair of weightlifter's dumbbells. If you stood on Pluto's surface, you would see Charon in the sky, three times as big as our Moon, but never moving.

- **In and out**
  Pluto has an elliptical orbit that every now and then swings it closer to the Sun than Neptune.

Comets and meteorites

PLANETS AND MOONS are not the only things whirling round the Sun. Along with the Earth and its companions are thousands upon thousands of tiny bits and pieces of rock and ice of all shapes and sizes. Some are smaller than a car. Others are several hundred kilometres across. These lumps of space debris are called asteroids. Every now and then, a very large lump of debris swings in from the outer limits of the solar system, creating a comet in the night sky. And all the time, lumps of this debris cannon into the Earth as meteors, some penetrating right through to the ground as meteorites.

FACTS: About asteroids

- **The asteroid belt**
  Asteroids are little chunks of debris that never clumped together to make a planet when the solar system was young. There are probably a million or more lying in a belt circling the Sun between Mars and Jupiter.

- **Ceres**
  The first of the asteroids to be spotted — and the biggest — is Ceres, as big as Ireland. The brightest is called Vesta, the only asteroid that can be seen with the naked eye.

- **The Trojan asteroids**
  The Trojans are two small groups of asteroids that circle the Sun on the same orbit as Jupiter.

▼ *Asteroids were first discovered in 1801, after a group of astronomers, calling themselves the Celestial Police, began hunting for a missing planet they were certain lay somewhere between Mars and Jupiter. Nowadays, new asteroids are discovered frequently. Each is given an identification number, and is named by the discoverer. Names vary from Greek goddesses to calculators.*

▲ *Every day, tons and tons of space debris rain down on the Earth, sometimes in such great concentrations that they make a golden rain in the night sky — called a meteor shower — as they hit the Earth's atmosphere and burn up. Meteors are space dust and lumps so small that they burn up long before they hit the ground. Meteorites are big enough to plunge right through the atmosphere and hit the ground. Most of these fall harmlessly into the oceans, and vary in size from lumps the size of shoes, to the meteorite the size of a car that hit Namibia, Africa, in 1920, creating an enormous crater.*

FACTS: About comets

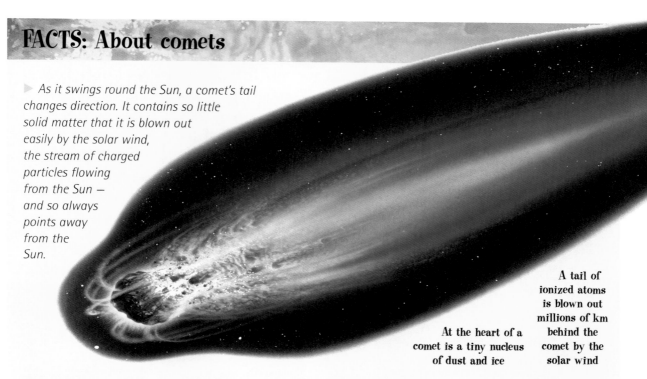

▶ As it swings round the Sun, a comet's tail changes direction. It contains so little solid matter that it is blown out easily by the solar wind, the stream of charged particles flowing from the Sun — and so always points away from the Sun.

A tail of ionized atoms is blown out millions of km behind the comet by the solar wind

At the heart of a comet is a tiny nucleus of dust and ice

- **Dirty snowballs**
  Comets with their flaming tails are the most spectacular sights in the night sky. But they are actually just dirty balls of ice, only a few kilometres across.

- **Visitors from afar**
  Many comets circle the Sun like the planets, but they have very long, stretched out orbits, and spend most of their time in the far reaches of the solar system. We see them only when their orbit brings them, for a few weeks, close to the Sun.

- **Glowing tails**
  The comet's tail is created as the comet hurtles towards the Sun and begins to melt. A vast plume of gas, millions of kilometres across, is blown out behind it by the solar wind, and this is what we see shining in the night as it catches the sunlight.

- **Periodics**
  Some comets, called Periodics, appear at regular intervals. Encke's comet comes every 1,206 days. Halley's comet comes every 76 years.

- **Speeding comets**
  Comets speed up as they near the Sun, sometimes reaching speeds of up to 2 million kmh. But far away from the Sun they slow down to speeds of little more than 1,000kmh, which is why they stay away for so long.

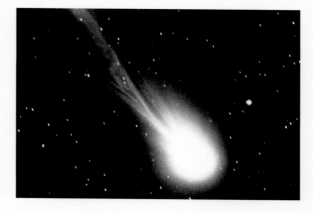

▲ Halley's comet, discovered by Edmund Halley (1656–1742), appeared before the Battle of Hastings in 1066, and some say it was the star of Bethlehem.

127

Stars

A star in close-up: our Sun

THE FEW THOUSAND STARS you see twinkling in the night sky are just a tiny fraction of the trillions scattered through the Universe. Like our Sun, they are huge fiery balls of hot gas. They shine because they are burning. Deep inside, atoms of gas fuse together in nuclear reactions that boost temperatures to millions of degrees, making their surfaces glow. A star goes on glowing, sending out light, heat, radio waves and radiation, until its nuclear fuel – mainly hydrogen gas – is used up.

FACTS: About giants and dwarfs

- **Giant stars**
  Most stars are much the same size as our Sun – about 1.4km across. But some are giants 100 times as big, or supergiants over 300 times as big.

- **Dwarf stars**
  Dwarf stars are actually very small – smaller than the Earth. Very old stars can shrink under the power of their own gravity to even tinier neutron stars – no bigger than the city of London, but so dense that they are as heavy as the Sun!

- **Starlight**
  The colour of starlight tells us what the star is made of, and how hot it is.

▲ The colour of a star depends on how bright it is. The Herzsprung-Russell diagram shows how the hotter and whiter stars glow, the brighter they are; the redder and cooler they glow, the dimmer they are. All medium-sized stars behave like this and form a band, called the Main Sequence stars, across the middle of the graph. Giants, dwarfs and neutron stars fall outside this band.

◀ Stars vary in brightness or 'magnitude'. The Herzsprung-Russell diagram shows how we expect stars of a certain colour to be a certain brightness, their Absolute Magnitude. But if a star is far away, it looks dimmer than expected. This is its Relative Magnitude.

▲ *Stars are being born and dying all over the Universe. The bigger the star, the shorter its life. The biggest stars end their lives in gigantic explosions called 'supernovae', which are, briefly, the brightest things in the night sky as incredibly hot gas billows away.*

FACTS: About constellations

- **Patterns in the stars**
  Ancient astronomers found their way around the heavens by looking for patterns of stars in the night sky. These patterns are called constellations. Astronomers now identify 88 of them, such as the Great Bear and Orion.

- **The Plough**
  The Plough, also known as the Great Bear or Ursa Major, is one of the best known constellations in the northern sky. It points towards the Pole Star, indicating north.

- **Alpha and beta**
  The stars in each constellation are named after letters in the Greek alphabet. The brightest star in each constellation is called Alpha, the next brightest Beta and so on. So Alpha Pegasi is the brightest star in Pegasus, the Flying Horse.

DATA: Stars

- **THE BRIGHTEST-LOOKING STAR**
  Sirius, the Dog Star, is the brightest star in the night sky. But it is quite nearby (8.6 light years) so its brightness is only relative.

- **THE BRIGHTEST STAR**
  Deneb burns as bright as 60,000 Suns but, because it is 1,800 light years away, it looks dimmer than Sirius.

- **THE BIGGEST STAR**
  No one knows what the biggest star is, but Antares is very big, 700 times as big as our Sun.

- **STARS WITH PLANETS LIKE THE SUN**
  At least nine other stars, including 51 Pegasi, are now known to have planets, like our Sun has.

▲ *Without constellations to help us, it would be hard to locate stars in the sky, but there is no real link between the stars in a constellation — they are completely imaginary patterns.*

Galaxies and nebulae

OUR SUN IS JUST ONE OF A MASSIVE collection of 2 billion stars arranged in a shape like a spinning fried egg. This gigantic collection of stars is called the Galaxy. It gets its name from the Greek for milky, because we see it as a milky white band across the night sky – called the Milky Way. But the Galaxy is just one of many millions of similar giant groups of stars, also called galaxies (with a small 'g'), scattered throughout the Universe.

▲ On a clear night, fuzzy patches of light can be seen amongst the stars. Some of these patches are distant galaxies. But others are huge clouds of dust called nebulae, many times bigger than any star. Only a few, called glowing nebulae, actually glow themselves; most are bright because the dust reflects starlight, just as clouds on Earth reflect sunlight. This picture show the famous Horsehead nebulae in the constellation of Orion, so-called because it is shaped a little like a horse's head.

FACTS: About galaxies

▶ *Spiral galaxies are spinning, Catherine wheel-shaped galaxies, like the Milky Way and Andromeda galaxies. They have a dense core of stars, surrounded by long whirling arms.*

▶ *Barred spiral galaxies are variations on spiral galaxies with a central bar from which arms of stars trail like water from a spinning garden sprinkler.*

▶ *Elliptical galaxies are huge egg-shaped galaxies sometimes containing a trillion stars. They are the oldest galaxies of all, some over 12 billion years old.*

▶ *Irregular galaxies are different from the others in that they have no obvious shape at all, and may have formed from the debris of colliding galaxies.*

▶ Stars start life in giant clouds of dust and gas called nebulae. Stars are born in these clouds as gravity pulls the dust into clumps — so ferociously that the pressure makes them glow.

- **Visible galaxies**
  Only three galaxies apart from the Milky Way can be seen with the naked eye: the Large and Small Magellanic Clouds and the Andromeda galaxy.

- **Far lights**
  Galaxies contain many millions of stars, each as big as our Sun. But they are so far away that, even with a reasonably good telescope, most look like blurs in the night sky. Andromeda, one of the nearest galaxies beyond the Milky Way, is over 3 million light-years away — 20 million trillion km!

- **The size of galaxies**
  Galaxies are absolutely gigantic. Although they contain millions or even trillions of stars, they are mostly empty space, for the stars are far apart. If each star was a person, the nearest neighbour would be almost as far away as the Moon.

- **How many galaxies?**
  Astronomers estimate that there are something like 20 trillion galaxies in the Universe.

- **Spiral galaxies**
  Just as the planets spin around the Sun, so spiral galaxies seem to be spinning too, which is why they have trailing arms.

- **Groups**
  Galaxies are often clustered in Groups of 30 or more. The Milky Way is part of the Local Group.

▶ The band of stars across the night sky called the Milky Way is an edge-on view of our own Galaxy, a vast cluster of stars 100,000 light years across. It is a spiral galaxy, and our Sun is just one of millions of stars on one of the trailing arms. As it whirls round, it sweeps the Sun (and with it the Earth) in a huge circle 100 million kilometres every hour. The Sun travels over 100,000 light years to go round once — and it will get round in 200 million years. So the dinosaurs had just appeared on Earth last time it was where it is now.

The Milky Way is 100,000 light years across and 1,000 light years thick.

Black holes

GRAVITY IS THE FORCE that holds the Universe together. It is the force that keeps the Earth in one piece, keeps us on the ground, and keeps planets circling the Sun and the stars together in galaxies. Yet it can also be so powerfully destructive that it can squeeze stars to nothing and suck galaxies into oblivion. When some giant stars burn out, there is nothing to hold them up and they start to collapse under the force of their own gravity. As they shrink, they get denser and denser, and their gravity becomes even stronger... and so they get denser and denser, and their gravity becomes stronger still. Eventually, they shrink to nothing... and if one goes on shrinking, it may create a hole in space, called a black hole.

FACTS: About gravity and orbits

- **Orbits**
  Things stay in orbit when their forward momentum exactly balances the pull of gravity.

- **The Earth's orbit**
  The Earth stays on the same path around the Sun because it is bowling through space too fast to be drawn in by the pull of the Sun — yet not so fast that it can overcome the Sun's pull altogether and hurtle off into space.

- **Satellites**
  Satellites seem to hang in space because they are moving too fast to fall into the Earth.

Launched too slow, the satellite falls back to Earth

Launched too fast, the satellite hurtles off into space

Launched at the right speed, the satellite goes into orbit

◀ A satellite has to be launched at exactly the right speed and on exactly the right trajectory (path) to be placed successfully in orbit. The lower the orbit is to be, the faster it must go if it is to avoid being pulled down by gravity. For an orbit 35,800km above the ground, the satellite has to be going fast enough to complete an orbit in exactly 24 hours — the same time it takes the Earth to spin. So a satellite placed in this orbit stays in the same place above the Earth.

◀ The destructive power of gravity can be seen on Jupiter's moon Io. The giant planet Jupiter is so massive that its gravity alternately pulls and sucks so powerfully on Io as it revolves that the insides of the moon get incredibly hot — so hot that volcanoes burst onto the surface.

FACTS: About the search for black holes

• **Do black holes exist?**
No one has ever seen a black hole. Indeed, we cannot be sure they actually exist. But the bright radiation from quasars (see below) — and from the centre of our galaxy may be signs that black holes do exist.

• **Where are black holes found?**
Some scientists think there is a giant black hole at the centre of each spiral galaxy. Some believe there are tiny ones everywhere.

◁ *This bright galaxy may have a black core.*

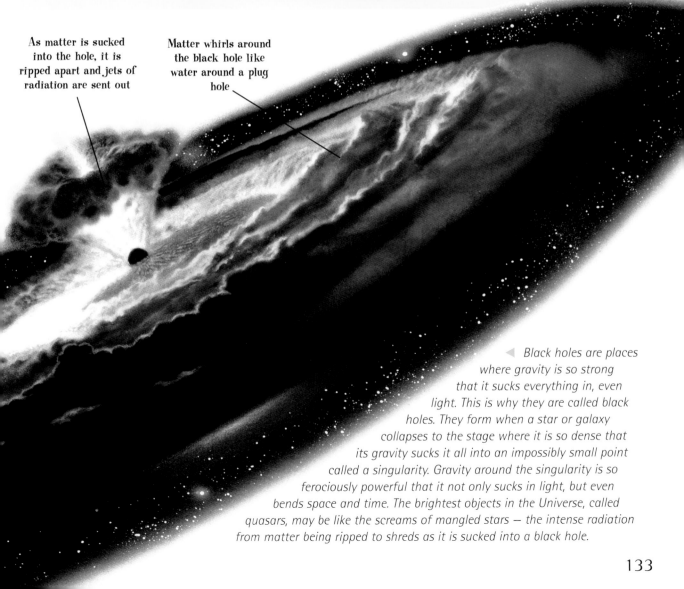

As matter is sucked into the hole, it is ripped apart and jets of radiation are sent out

Matter whirls around the black hole like water around a plug hole

◁ *Black holes are places where gravity is so strong that it sucks everything in, even light. This is why they are called black holes. They form when a star or galaxy collapses to the stage where it is so dense that its gravity sucks it all into an impossibly small point called a singularity. Gravity around the singularity is so ferociously powerful that it not only sucks in light, but even bends space and time. The brightest objects in the Universe, called quasars, may be like the screams of mangled stars — the intense radiation from matter being ripped to shreds as it is sucked into a black hole.*

133

How far to the stars?

 THE UNIVERSE IS VERY, VERY BIG. In fact, the distances between the stars are so huge that astronomers don't measure them in kilometres, but in light years – which is how far light travels in a year. Light is the fastest thing in the Universe and travels at about 300,000km per second, so a light year is 9,460 billion kms. The nearest star is 4.3 light years away. The most distant objects so far discovered – very bright galaxies called quasars – are over 13 billion light years away. That means that light takes over 13 billion years to reach us – so astronomers are looking at them as they were 13 billion years ago!

DATA: Distances in space

- **THE NEAREST PLANET**
  The nearest planet to Earth is Venus, which is over 40 million km away.

- **THE FURTHEST PLANET**
  The furthest planet from Earth in the solar system is Pluto, which is nearly 6 billion km away.

- **THE NEAREST STAR**
  The nearest star is Proxima Centauri, in the constellation of the Centaur, which is 4.3 light years away, or about 40 trillion km away.

- **THE NEAREST OUTSIDE GALAXY**
  The nearest galaxy outside our own is the Andromeda galaxy, 2.5 million light years – over 20 billion billion km away.

- **THE FURTHEST GALAXY**
  The furthest galaxy yet seen is over 13 billion light years away across the Universe – over 12 billion trillion km away.

- **DISTANCE TO THE MOON**
  At its nearest, the Moon is 356,410km away; at its furthest, 406,697km.

- **DISTANCE TO THE SUN**
  At its nearest, the Sun is 147 million km away; at its furthest, over 152 million km.

- **PARSECS**
  Astronomers may measure large distances in parsecs. A parsec is 3.26 light years. Parsec distances are worked out by using the geometry of 'parallaxes' – the way a star seems to shift slightly in position in the night sky as the Earth moves around the Sun.

Distances in space are vast

◄ The distance to the Moon is measured to within a few metres by bouncing laser beams off mirrors left on the Moon by astronauts.

FACTS: Galactic distances

- **Standard candles**
  To find the distance of a nearby galaxy, astronomers look for stars within it whose brightness they are sure of. These include stars called 'cepheid variables', 'supergiant stars' and giant exploding stars called 'supernova'.

- **Very distant galaxies**
  Astronomers cannot pick out individual stars in very distant galaxies, so they estimate the distance by tricks such as the Tully-Fisher technique, based on how it appears to be spinning. The faster it spins, the brighter it should be. So if it is dim, it must be far away.

- **Red shift**
  The redder a distant galaxy looks, the faster it is moving away from us.

► The distance to the Sun and nearby planets is measured by bouncing radar beams off them. Space probes help with planets further away.

► Distances to the nearer stars are generally worked out either by the parallax method (see parsecs) or by estimating their brightness. Astronomers can guess how bright a star should look compared to other stars from its colour. If it actually looks brighter than it should, it must be nearby; if it looks dimmer, it must be further away.

▼ Distances to the galaxies are worked out by looking for 'standard candles', stars whose brightness we can be sure of. Really far off galaxies call for even more ingenious methods.

Working out distances

The method astronomers use to work out the distance of an object in space depends on how far away it is. For nearby objects such as the Sun and the planets, they can use radar beams, and estimates can be accurate within a few thousand km. They measure distances to nearby stars by gauging their brightness, and estimates are accurate only to within a few billion km. Distances to far galaxies are accurate only to within a few billion light years!

Space travel

THE AGE OF SPACE EXPLORATION began in 1957 when powerful rocket engines boosted the Russian satellite Sputnik 1 free of the Earth's gravity. This was the start of an extraordinary series of adventures for mankind which has seen scores of satellites put in space, man's first steps on the Moon, live broadcasts from Mars and space probes venturing past the outer planets of the solar system. These probes have not only beamed back the first pictures of new previously unknown moons but have also provided remarkable insights into the nature of the Universe.

FACTS: About spacecraft

- **Rocket power**
  Very powerful rockets are needed to push a spacecraft clear of the Earth's gravity — but once clear, such power is no longer needed. So rockets are made in separate stages, each of which falls away when its fuel is spent.

- **The space shuttle**
  In the early days, manned spacecraft could be used only once, with just a tiny capsule holding the astronauts falling back to the Earth at the end of the mission. The US space shuttle was the first spacecraft that could be reused, landing back on the Earth like an aeroplane. The boosters that launch it into space are recovered.

- **Space probes**
  Unmanned space probes, guided by computer, have now visited all the planets but Pluto, the smallest and most distant, and probes have actually landed on Mars and Venus. Late in 1997, the Mars Pathfinder beamed back live pictures from the surface of Mars.

- **Slingshot effect**
  Space probes voyaging to the planets use gravity to help them travel huge distances on very little fuel. As they pass each planet, their gravity pulls them in and hurls them onwards on a slightly different course, like a slingshot.

▲ *The space shuttle is launched with solid fuel booster rockets that fall away but are then recovered. Typical shuttle missions include launching and repairing satellites and performing scientific experiments.*

FACTS: About satellites and probes

- **Staying in orbit**
  Satellites stay in space because they are circling, or 'orbiting', the Earth just too fast to be pulled down by Earth's gravity — but not so fast that they fly off into space.

- **Staying still**
  An orbit 35,800km above the ground takes exactly 24 hours — the same time it takes the Earth to spin once. So satellites on this orbit stay in exactly the same place above the Earth. This is called a geostationary orbit.

- **Hubble space telescope**
  Satellites not only give a clear view of the Earth from space, but a better view of space too, because they are free from Earth's atmosphere. The Hubble space telescope, launched in 1990, gives extraordinary pictures of distant objects in space.

▲ *Spacecraft can be remarkably ungainly looking objects. Once they are free of the Earth's atmosphere, there is no need for streamlining, and aerials and dishes stick out in all directions. This is the Galileo launched in 1989 to explore Jupiter.*

DATA: Milestones in space exploration

- **THE FIRST LIVING CREATURE IN SPACE**
  Laika the dog was launched in the Russian *Sputnik 2* in November 1957. Sadly she could not be brought back.

- **THE FIRST MAN IN SPACE**
  The first man in space was the Russian cosmonaut Yuri Gagarin, in April 1961.

- **THE FIRST SPACE WALK**
  In 1965, Russian cosmonaut Alexei Leonov was the first man to walk in space.

- **THE FIRST MEN ON THE MOON**
  The American *Apollo* astronauts Neil Armstrong and Buzz Aldrin stepped on the Moon on 21 July 1969.

- **REACHING VENUS**
  In 1970, the Soviet Union's *Venera 7* landed on Venus.

- **PASSING SATURN**
  In 1969, the US *Pioneer II* probe reached Saturn and discovered new moons.

- **REACHING NEPTUNE**
  In 1989, the US *Voyager 2* reached the planet Neptune.

- **MARS LANDING**
  In 1997, the Mars Pathfinder roved the surface of Mars, beaming back pictures.

137

History of the Universe

THE UNIVERSE PROBABLY BEGAN about 13 billion years ago. One moment there was nothing. The next there was a minute, unimaginably hot ball – and suddenly the Universe burst into existence with the biggest explosion of all time, called the Big Bang, swelling at a totally astonishing rate. This explosion was so big that everything is still hurtling away from it, which is why the Universe is expanding. Even now, 13 billion years on, astronomers can detect the faint afterglow, called the cosmic microwave background radiation, spread throughout the night sky.

FACTS: Expanding universe

- **Receding galaxies**
  As astronomers observe space, they can see galaxies zooming away from us in all directions at astonishing speeds. The further they are away, the faster they seem to be moving. This can only mean the Universe is expanding.

- **The Big Crunch?**
  Some scientists think the Universe will go on expanding forever. This is called the 'open universe' idea. Others think gravity will put a break on its expansion. If there is a great deal of dark matter — matter we can't detect — it may be enough to make it all start to shrink again. Then it may end in a Big Crunch.

▶ *We know how fast galaxies are receding because of the colour of light from them. The faster they are receding, the more light waves from them get stretched out. When light waves are stretched they look redder. This is called red shift. The redder the light, the faster the galaxy is moving away.*

FACTS: About how the solar system was born

- **Swirling cloud**
  4.6 billion years ago, the solar system did not exist. There was just a hot, dark cloud of gases swirling round the Sun. The planets began to form as the cloud cooled and droplets began to clump together.

- **The birth of the Earth**
  The Earth probably formed as gravity began to pull together clumps of star dust from around the Sun. But this early Earth was a molten ball.

▼ *No one knows where the material that formed the solar system came from. Some think it was the remnants of an exploded star, others the result of a collision between stars.*

◄ *Scientists have worked out how the Universe began by mathematical calculations and experiments with huge machines called particle accelerators, which hurl atoms together. It started with a tiny hot ball which cooled to 10 billion billion billion°C as it grew to the size of a football. In a split second, it swelled to create a space bigger than a galaxy in a period called inflation. Within this space, all the matter and energy and forces began to take the form we know in the Universe today. At first, it was a dense chaotic soup of particles and energy. But then atoms began to form, and the atoms formed clouds, and the clouds galaxies.*

139

Key facts: The Universe

The planets

Planet	Diameter (km)	Av. distance from Sun (million km)	Rotation period	Length of year	Tilt of axis	Mass, if Earth =1	Brightness
Mercury	4,878	57.91	58.65 days	87.97 days	2°	0.055	-1.9
Venus	12,102	108.2	243.01 days	224.7 days	177.3°	0.815	-4.4
Earth	12,756	149.6	23.93 hours	365.26 days	23.45°	1	
Mars	6,786	227.9	24.62 hrs	686.98 days	25.19°	0.107	-2.0
Jupiter	142,984	778.3	9.84 hrs	11.86 years	3.1°	317.94	-2.7
Saturn	120,536	1,427	10.23 hrs	29.46 yrs	26.7°	95.18	+0.7
Uranus	51,118	2,871	17.9 hrs	84.01 yrs	98°	14.53	+5.5
Neptune	49,528	4,497	19.2 hrs	164.79 yrs	29.6°	17.14	+7.8
Pluto	2,300	5,914	6.39 hrs	248.54 yrs	122.5°	0.002	+15.1

Milestones

- AD 140: Ptolemy devises his model of the motion of the planets and stars.
- 1543: Nicolaus Copernicus shows that the planets revolve around the Sun, not the Earth.
- 1610: Galileo uses a telescope to see things such as the phases of Venus and the moons of Jupiter.
- 1659: Christiaan Huygens discovers the rings of Saturn.
- 1781: William Herschel discovers the planet Uranus.
- 1801: Giuseppi Piazzi discovers Ceres, the first asteroid.
- 1846: John Galle discovers the planet Neptune.
- 1929: Edwin Hubble shows that there are other galaxies beyond our own and that the Universe is expanding.
- 1930: Clyde Tombaugh discovers the planet Pluto.
- 1978: James Christy finds Pluto's moon Charon.
- 1995: Michael Mayer and Didier Queloz spot a planet circling the star 51 Pegasi.

The constellations

Andromeda
Antlia, the Air Pump
Apus, the Bird of Paradise
Aquarius, the Water-Bearer
Aquila, the Eagle
Ara, the Altar
Aries, the Ram
Auriga, the Charioteer
Boötes, the Herdsman
Caelum, the Graving Tool
Camelopardalis, the Giraffe
Cancer, the Crab
Canes Venatici, the Hunting
   Dogs
Canis Major, the Great Dog
Canis Minor, the Little Dog
Capricornus, the Sea Goat
Carina, the Keel
Cassiopeia
Centaurus, the Centaur
Cepheus
Cetus, the Whale
Chamaeleon, the Chameleon
Circinus, the Compasses
Columba, the Dove
Coma Berenices, Berenice's
   Hair
Corona Australis, Southern
   Crown
Corona Borealis, the Northern
   Crown
Corvus, the Crow
Crater, the Cup
Crux, the Southern Cross
Cygnus, the Swan
Delphinius, the Dolphin
Dorado, the Swordfish
Draco, the Dragon
Equuleus, the Foal

Eridanus
Fornax, the Furnace
Gemini, the Twins
Grus, the Crane
Hercules
Horologium, the Clock
Hydra, the Water Snake
Hydrus, the Little Snake
Indus, the Indian
Lacerta, the Lizard
Leo, the Lion
Leo Minor, the Little Lion
Lepus, the Hair
Libra, the Scales of Justice
Lupus, the Wolf
Lynx, the Lynx
Lyra, the Lyre
Mensa, the Table
Microscopium, the Microscope
Monoceros, the Unicorn
Musca, the Fly
Norma, the Rule
Octans, the Octant
Ophiuchus, the Serpent-Bearer
Orion
Pavo, the Peacock
Pegasus, the Flying Horse
Perseus

Phoenix, the Phoenix
Pictor, the Painter
Pisces, the Fishes
Piscis Austrinus, the Southern
   Fish
Puppis, the Poop
Pyxis, the Compass
Reticulum, the Net
Sagitta, the Arrow
Sagittarius, the Archer
Scorpius, the Scorpion
Sculptor, the Sculptor
Scutum, the Shield
Serpens, the Serpent
Sextans, the Sextant
Taurus, the Bull
Telescopium, the Telescope
Triangulum, the Triangle
Triangulum Australe, the
   Southern Triangle
Tucana, the Toucan
Ursa Major, the Great Bear
Ursa Minor, the Little Bear
Vela, the Sails
Virgo, the Virgin
Volans, the Flying Fish
Vulpecula, the Fox

Moons of the planets

Earth's moon
- The Moon

Mars's moons
- Phobos
- Deimos

Jupiter's moons
- Metis
- Adastrea
- Amalthea
- Thebe
- Io
- Europa
- Ganymede
- Callisto
- Leda
- Himalia
- Lysithea
- Elara
- Ananke
- Carme

- Pasiphae
- Sinope
- Phoebe

Saturn's moons
- Unnamed
- Pan
- Atlas
- Prometheus
- Pandora
- Janus
- Epimetheus
- Mimas
- Enceladus
- Tethys
- Telesto
- Calypso
- Dione
- Helene
- Rhea
- Titan

- Hyperion
- Iapetus
- Phoebe

Uranus's moons
- Cordelia
- Ophelia
- Bianca
- Cressida
- Desdemona
- Juliet
- Portia
- Rosalind
- Belinda
- Puck
- Ariel
- Umbriel
- Titania
- Oberon

Neptune's moons
- Naiad
- Thalassa
- Despina
- Galatea
- Larissa
- Proteus
- Triton
- Neraid

Pluto's moon
- Charon

Saturn, with 19 moons, has more moons than any other planet in our solar system.

Nearest and brightest stars

Nearest stars
- Sun (0.0 light years away from Earth)
- Proxima Centauri (4.2)
- Alpha Centauri A (4.3)
- Alpha Centauri B (4.3)
- Barnard's star (5.9)
- Wolf 359 (7.6)
- Lalance 21185 (8.1)
- Sirius A (8.6)
- Sirius B (8.6)
- UV Ceti A (8.9)

Brightest stars
- Sun (0.0-light years away from Earth)
- Sirius A (8.6)
- Canopus (200)
- Alpha Centauri (4.3)

- Arcturus (36)
- Vega (26)
- Capella (42)
- Rigel (910)
- Procyon (11)
- Achernar (85)

Space exploration

- **1926** The American engineer Robert Goddard designed and launched the first liquid fuel rocket.
- **1942** Wernher von Braun developed the V2 rocket in Nazi Germany.
- **1957** The world's first artificial satellite, the USSR's *Sputnik 1*, was launched.
- **1957** The Russian dog Laika became the first living creature in space aboard *Sputnik 2*.
- **1961** The Soviet cosmonaut Yuri Gagarin became the first man in space aboard *Vostok 1*.
- **1963** The Soviet cosmonaut Valentina Tereshkova became the first woman in space.
- **1966** The USSR's unmanned probe *Lunar 9* landed on the Moon.
- **1969** US astronauts Neil Armstrong and Edwin Aldrin were the first men to walk on the Moon.
- **1972** *Apollo 17* was the sixth and last US manned mission to the Moon.
- **1973** First US space station *Skylab* launched.

- **1980** The US *Voyager 1* took the first detailed photos of Saturn's ring systems and discovered six additional moons.
- **1981** The US space shuttle *Columbia*, the world's first reusable spacecraft, was launched.
- **1982** The Soviet probe *Venera 13* sent back colour photos of the surface of Venus.
- **1986** The shuttle programme was halted for several years after the shuttle *Challenger* exploded, killing its crew of seven.
- **1990** The Hubble space telescope was launched.
- **1996** US scientists found evidence in meteor fragments that microbes may have existed on Mars.

Quiz: The Universe

1. The Earth is 40,000km round at the equator: true or false?

2. There is water on the Moon: true or false?

3. The footprints left by the astronauts on the Moon in the 1960s are still there: true or false?

4. How big are the smallest sunspots - as big as Africa or 50 times as big as Africa?

5. On what is the SOHO space telescope targeted?

6. A light year is the distance light travels in a year: true or false?

7. Who was the first man in space?

8. What did Neil Armstrong say when he stepped onto the Moon?

9. How many manned missions to the Moon were there - six or 22?

10. Who was the first man to walk in space?

11. What is the launch path of a satellite called?

12. What is the name of the space probe that landed on Mars in 1997?

13. Mercury has ice caps of acid: true or false?

14. Which planet is closest to the Earth?

15. Which of the planets in the solar system has the shortest year?

16. Are there volcanoes on Venus?

17. Which planet is furthest from the Sun?

18. Saturn would float if you could find a bath big enough: true or false?

19. The surface of Jupiter is spinning at 45,000 kmh: true or false?

20. Comets are made mostly of ice: true or false?

Answers:

1. True
2. True
3. True
4. 50 times as big as Africa
5. The Sun
6. True
7. Yuri Gagarin in 1961
8. 'That's one small step for man, one giant leap for mankind.'
9. Six
10. Alexei Leonov in 1965
11. Its trajectory
12. Mars Pathfinder
13. True
14. Venus
15. Mercury (88 days)
16. Yes
17. Pluto
18. True
19. True
20. True

PLANET EARTH

Home planet

THE EARTH MAY SEEM QUITE STILL but it is actually spinning round like a top at over 800km an hour – faster than most jet planes. It is also hurtling through the dark on its orbit around the Sun at over 100,000kmh! Every year it covers 939,886,400km in its orbit round the Sun. The Earth's entire journey around the Sun takes exactly 365.242 days, which is why there are 365 days in our year. We make up the extra 0.242 days in our calendar by an extra day every fourth year, called a leap year – then miss out a leap three centuries out of four.

FACTS: About latitude and longitude

▲ Lines of latitude are called parallels because they form rings around the Earth parallel to the equator, which is latitude 0°. The North Pole is latitude 90°N.

▲ Lines of longitude or meridians run around the Earth from pole to pole, dividing the world up like the segments of an orange.

- **Lines of latitude**
  Every place on the Earth's surface can be pinpointed by two figures: its latitude and longitude. Lines of equal latitude (called parallels) form rings around the Earth parallel to the equator. A place's latitude is given in degrees north or south of the equator.

- **Lines of longitude**
  Lines of longitude (called meridians) run around the Earth from north to south. A place's longitude is given as degrees west or east of the Prime Meridian which runs through Greenwich in London, England.

In spring, north and south get equal sun

When the north is tilted away from the Sun, it is winter here, but summer in the south

When the north is tilted towards the Sun, it is summer here, but winter in the south

In autumn, north and south get equal sun

▲ We get seasons because the Earth is always tilted over in the same direction. So when the Earth is on one side of the Sun, the northern hemisphere (the world north of the equator) is tilted towards the Sun, bringing summer here. At this time, the southern hemisphere is tilted away, and so gets winter. When the Earth is on the other side of the Sun, the northern hemisphere is tilted away, bringing winter, while the south gets summer.

DATA: Our home planet

- DISTANCE OF THE EARTH FROM THE SUN
  The Earth is 149.6 million km from the Sun. At its nearest, called the perihelion, it is 147,097,800km away. At its furthest (the aphelion), on 4 July, it is 152,098,200km away.

- SPIN TIME
  The Earth spins round once every 23 hours 56 mins and 4.09 seconds. The Sun appears to come back to the same place in the sky once every 24 hours.

FACTS: About the time of day

- Time zones
  As the Earth spins, the Sun is always rising in one place and setting in another. So the time of day varies around the world. When it's dawn where you live, it's sunset on the other side of the world. To make it easier to set clocks, the world is split into 24 time zones, one for each hour of the day. As you go east around the world, you put clocks forward by one hour for each zone — until you reach a line called the International Date Line. If you carry on across the Date Line, you carry on adding hours, but put the calendar a day back.

▲ Half the world is facing the Sun and is brightly lit; the other half is facing away and in darkness. As the Earth spins round on its axis, the dark and sunlit halves move around, bringing day and night around the world. Because the Earth is turning eastwards, the Sun appears from the ground to come up in the east and sink again in the west. The Earth turns once every 24 hours, which is why days are 24 hours long.

The Earth's atmosphere

WRAPPED AROUND the Earth is a thin blanket of gases called the atmosphere. This blanket is no thicker on the Earth than the peel on an apple. Yet without it, the Earth would be as lifeless as the Moon. It gives us the air we need to breathe. It gives us clean water to drink. And it keeps us warm by trapping the Sun's heat – yet at the same time shielding us from the most harmful of its rays. It gives us weather, too, for everything we call weather is the churning of the atmosphere's lowest layer, next to the ground, as it is stirred by the Sun's warmth.

FACTS: About water in the air

- **Water cycle**
  All the water on the Earth is forever being recycled in a process called the water cycle (see below).

- **Watery planet**
  Over 70 per cent of the Earth's surface is covered by water. At any one time, though, just 1 per cent is in the atmosphere. 97 percent is in the oceans. The rest is in lakes and rivers or frozen as ice.

- **Humidity**
  The air is full of invisible water vapour. The amount of water vapour in the air at any one time is known as its humidity.

- **Relative humidity**
  The total amount of moisture in the air is its 'absolute' humidity. But the warmer air is, the more water it can hold, so meteorologists look at 'relative' humidity, or rh, which is the percentage of moisture actually in the air relative to the maximum it could hold at that temperature.

- **Turning to water**
  As air cools, its rh must go up, because cool air can hold less moisture. Eventually, the rh reaches 100 per cent and the vapour condenses into drops of water. This is called the dew point.

Clouds drop rain and snow on the land

Water falling on the land runs in rivers back to the sea

Water evaporated from the oceans forms clouds

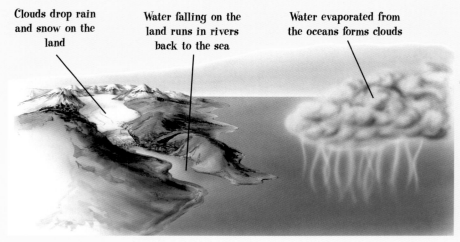

◁ The Sun's heat makes water evaporate from the oceans and rise into the air. As it rises, it cools off and condenses into tiny drops of water, forming clouds. When the drops get big enough, they fall as rain or snow back into the oceans – or onto the land where the water runs in rivers back to the sea again.

► The atmosphere all looks like thin air, but scientists have shown that it has five or more layers or 'spheres', each with its own characteristics. We live in the lowest layer, called the troposphere. This layer is just 12km thick, but 75 per cent of the atmosphere's gases sink into this layer. As you go higher and higher, the gases get more and more spread out until by the time you are 1,000 kilometres or so up, the gases are so thin or 'rarefied' that the atmosphere fades off into space.

FACTS: About air pressure

▲ Air pressure can be measured on a device called a barometer. Barometers help tell you if a storm is on its way, because storms are linked to low pressure. If the pressure drops sharply, you can be sure rain and wind are on their way.

- **Atmospheric pressure**
  At sea level, the atmosphere is so dense that there is a crush of air molecules. This crush creates enormous pressure in the air, called atmospheric or air pressure.

- **Wind and pressure**
  Air pressure varies from time to time and place to place. High pressure pushes air towards zones of high pressure, and this is what creates winds — air moving from high pressure to low pressure zones. The sharper the pressure difference, the stronger the wind.

Satellite

Eventually the atmosphere fades into the vacuum of space

Exosphere (up to 700km): the gases are very rarefied

Thermosphere (up to 300km): is even thinner in gases, but is heated by the Sun to over 2,000°C

Higher level aurora

Comet

Lower level aurora

Mesosphere (up to 80km): is too thin in gases to soak up much heat so it is very cold, down to -120°C

Radio waves bounce off ionosphere

Stratosphere (up to 50km): gets hotter higher up. Airliners cruise in the still air

Ultraviolet rays

Troposphere (up to 12km): 70% of the gases and all the weather is here. It gets cooler higher up

800km
700km
600km
500km
400km
300km
200km
100km 80km 50km
12km
0km

151

Weather

THERE ARE MANY DIFFERENT KINDS OF WEATHER – rain, snow, sun, wind, fog, mist, frost. But all of them are simply changes in the air caused by the varying effect of the Sun's warmth. Winds blow up, for instance, when the Sun heats some places more than others, setting the air moving. Rain falls when air warmed by the Sun lifts moisture high enough for it to form big drops of water when it condenses. Frost and snow occur when the power of the Sun is reduced. All weather comes down to three factors: the way the air moves (wind), its moisture content (humidity) and its temperature (warmth).

FACTS: About thunderstorms

- **Thunder clouds**

  Huge thunderclouds are built up by strong updraughts on a hot day or along a cold front. Eddies in the cloud hurl water drops and ice together so hard they become charged with static electricity (see p183). Positive particles clustering at the top of the cloud, and negative particles at the bottom, create a charge difference. Soon the charge difference builds up so much that lightning flashes from positive to negative.

▼ *Fork lightning flashes from cloud to ground. Sheet lightning flashes within the cloud. Lightning heats the air so much it bursts in a clap of thunder.*

Fronts

The stormiest weather in many places is linked to depressions (low pressure regions). A wedge of warm air intrudes into the heart of depressions, and the worst weather occurs along the edges of this wedge, called fronts, where the warm air meets the cold. As the depression moves over, the fronts bring a distinct sequence of weather.

Cold front

▲ *Once the warm front has passed, the weather becomes milder and clearer for a while. But after a few hours, a build-up of thunderclouds and gusts of wind warn that the trailing edge of the wedge, called the cold front, is on its way. As the cold front passes over, the thunderclouds unleash short but heavy rain showers, and even thunderstorms, before calm returns.*

FACTS: About clouds and rain

- **Making clouds**
  Clouds form when water vapour rises with warm air then condenses as the air cools in the upper air. It rains when the water drops in clouds get too heavy to float on the air.

- **Icy rain**
  Most rain comes from water droplets freezing into ice particles in a cloud. The particles grow into snowflakes, then melt into raindrops as they fall — or stay as snow if the air is cold.

- **Tropical rain**
  In the tropics, raindrops form inside tall clouds as small raindrops join up to make bigger drops heavy enough to fall as rain.

◁ *Rain clouds are grey because they are so thick with large drops of water that they block out the sunlight.*

▽ *Natural snowflakes are six-sided and consist of crystals that are mostly flat plates, but can be needles or columns. Under a magnifying glass, you can see that no two snowflakes are ever the same.*

Warm front

▲ *First to arrive is the leading edge of the wedge of warm air, or warm front, where warm air slides over cold air. As it rises it forms banks of clouds along the front. So the coming of the warm front is heralded by feathery 'cirrus' clouds high in the sky. Soon the clouds thicken until the sky is full of slate-grey 'nimbostratus' clouds, which bring long periods of steady rain.*

DATA: Weather

- **WETTEST**
  The wettest place in the world is Tutunendo in Columbia which gets 1,170cm of rain anually – 20 times as much as London.

- **THE COLDEST AND HOTTEST**
  The coldest place is Vostok in Antarctica where it averages -57.8°C. The hottest is Dallol in Ethiopia, where it averages 34°C in the shade, and can get much hotter.

153

Wind

ALL WIND IS SIMPLY AIR MOVING. Strong winds are air moving fast. Gentle breezes are air moving slowly. Air moves because the Sun warms some places more than others, creating differences in air pressure which push the air about. Warmth makes the air expand and rise, lowering air pressure. But where the air is cold and heavy, air pressure is high. Winds blow from areas where pressure is high, called anticyclones, to areas where pressure is low, called cyclones or depressions. The sharper the difference in pressure, the stronger the wind is.

FACTS: About hurricanes

◀ Every summer, nine or so hurricanes develop in the eastern Atlantic and spiral westwards to the Gulf of Mexico, tracked all the way by satellite. Here a hurricane's distinctive spiral of clouds is seen hitting the coast of Texas.

▶ Hurricanes are shaped like huge spiral cakes. Winds spiralling in towards the low pressure centre, or eye, help line the thunderclouds into great walls of cloud towering into the sky.

- **Hurricanes and typhoons**
  Hurricanes are the Atlantic version of the cyclone storms that batter eastern coasts in the tropics. In the Pacific they are known as typhoons.

- **What a hurricane does**
  When a hurricane strikes, trees can be ripped up and buildings flattened by winds gusting up to 360kmh. Vast areas can be battered and swamped by torrential rain, and coasts can be completely overwhelmed by the 'storm surge' — the mound of sea water that builds up in the storm centre.

- **Hurricane year**
  There are on average 103 typhoons and other tropical storms and 45 hurricanes every year.

- **How hurricanes start**
  Hurricanes begin in the eastern Atlantic as thunderstorms set off by moist air rising over the warm ocean. If the water is warm enough, they pile up together, then begin to spiral westwards across the ocean, growing bigger all the time.

- **Gaining power**
  By the time the hurricane has crossed the Atlantic, it is spiralling tighter and tighter round its centre or 'eye'. The eye shrinks to just 50km across and winds howl round it at over 120kmh.

FACTS: About tornadoes

• **Twisters**
Tornadoes are tiny spirals of wind that sweep past in less than 15 minutes — but 300kmh winds and a low pressure centre that sucks like a giant vacuum cleaner can toss people, cars and buildings high in the air like toys. They are common from March to July in 'Tornado Alley' in the Midwest of the USA.

• **Supercells**
Tornadoes are set off by giant thunderclouds called supercells. Winds whipping through the clouds set updraughts spinning. As they spin, they create a vortex which hangs from the cloud base down to the ground, like an elephant's trunk.

▲ *Often it is the torrential rain and the storm surge of ocean water that do most of the damage in a hurricane, but the ferocious winds can also wreak havoc, blowing down trees and buildings.*

• **The eye**
The air in the dead centre or eye of the hurricane is at very low pressure, and is very calm. As the eye passes over, the winds may drop altogether and a small circle of blue sky may often be seen. But the lull is short-lived, for the rain and wind are at their strongest either side of the eye.

• **Big wind**
A hurricane can be 800km across, and it can take 18 hours to pass over.

• **Hurricane warning.**
Each hurricane is given a name and tracked by satellite to help give people plenty of warning that one is on its way.

Dry air sinks in the eye

Warm, moist air spirals around the eye

Air rises, building up huge thunderclouds

Calm eye of storm, where winds drop and pressure is very low

Air drawn in towards the low pressure at the centre of the storm

Structure of the Earth

THE EARTH IS NOT QUITE THE SOLID BALL it seems. Using sensitive equipment to detect the pattern of vibrations from earthquakes and big explosions, scientists have shown it has quite a complicated structure. Only a very thin shell, called the crust, is completely solid. Inside are a number of different layers, some solid, but some soft like thick treacle, while some of the core is molten metal. Atomic reactions in the core mean the Earth gets hotter and hotter as you go deeper towards the centre, reaching over 7,000°C in the centre – hotter than the surface of the Sun.

FACTS: Inside the Earth

- **Thin crust**
  The Earth's crust of rock is on average 40km thick under the continents and just 6km beneath the oceans.

- **Soft mantle**
  Beneath the crust is the mantle, nearly 3,000km thick and made of rock so warm it flows like treacle, only very, very slowly.

- **Metal core**
  In the centre of the Earth is a core of metal (iron with a little nickel). The outer core is so hot it is molten. The inner core is even hotter, but pressures are so great the metal stays solid.

- **Crust edge**
  The boundary between the crust and mantle is called the Mohorovicic discontinuity.

- **Rigid top**
  The very top of the mantle is stiff and attached to the crust, so that they move as one – so scientists sometimes talk of the 'lithosphere', which is the crust and the top of the mantle down to 100km.

- **Soft underneath**
  Beneath the lithosphere in the upper mantle is the softer 'asthenosphere' down to 200km, where rock circulates very slowly.

▲ The world is a bit like a partly boiled egg, with a hard shell or crust, a white of semi-soft rock called the mantle, and a yolk or core of molten and solid metal.

- **Lower down**
  Below the asthenosphere is a third, stiffer layer within the upper mantle, called the mesosphere.

- **Mesophere**
  Heat makes the whole of the mantle churn very slowly, over millions of years. Sometimes big hot blobs rise right up from the core to the crust. These 'superplumes' may create huge volcanoes.

▲ *The pulling apart of tectonic plates creates giant cracks in the Earth's surface. Usually, these cracks are hidden underwater on the ocean bed. But in Iceland, the crack which runs right down the middle of the Atlantic ocean bed comes to the surface. Each side of this valley is a different plate, and they are slowly pulling apart.*

▼ *The giant plates that make up the Earth's hard shell or lithosphere are always moving, although very, very slowly. In some places, plates are crunching together, and one of the plates — typically a continent — rides over the other and forces it down into the Earth's interior. This process is called subduction. In other places — usually in mid-ocean on the seabed — plates are pulling apart. But, even as they pull apart, so they gain new material as hot molten rock wells up through the gap and solidifies on the exposed edges. This is called mid-ocean spreading.*

FACTS: Moving plates

- **Tectonic plates**
  The Earth's rocky crust is broken into 20 or so huge fragments called tectonic plates. As these move slowly about, they set off earthquakes and volcanoes, and pile up mountain ranges.

- **Continental drift**
  As tectonic plates move, they carry the continents slowly about the world.

▼ *The Earth's crust is broken into 20 or so plates which carry continents as they move. Africa and South America were once joined. Europe is drifting slowly further from America.*

In the middle of the ocean, where plates are pulling apart, new molten rock wells up to create a series of ridges under the sea

Deep trench in the ocean where a plate is subducted

Ocean

Subducted plate pushed into the Earth's interior

In 'subduction zones' plates are pushing together, pushing one plate beneath the other

Rock from the melting plate burns up to erupt through as volcanoes

Continent

Molten rock from the mantle

Plates pulling apart

Lithosphere

Asthenosphere

Plates pushing together

Subducted plate melting

History of the Earth

THE EARTH probably formed about 4.6 billion years ago from debris spinning round the Sun. At first, it was a molten ball, but it gradually cooled and a thin crust formed around the outside. The first signs of life – probably bacteria – appeared nearly 4 billion years ago. But the first animals with shells and bones easily preserved as fossils did not appear until about 600 million years ago. It is mainly with the help of such fossils that geologists have built up a picture of the Earth's history since then. Very little is known about the 4 billion years before this, called Precambrian time.

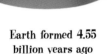

Earth formed 4.55 billion years ago

Archean 4,600-2,500 million years ago (m.y.a.)

▲ *This spiral shows some events in the Earth's history, starting with its origin at the centre of the spiral and the coming of humans at the end. The scale is distorted because so little is known about what happened in the first 85 per cent of the Earth's history – so the last 15 per cent is given much more space. If Earth's history were crammed into a day, humans would appear only at the end, just two seconds before midnight.*

FACTS: Geological time

- **Units of time**
  Just as the day is divided into hours, minutes and seconds, so geologists divide the Earth's history into time periods. The longest are Eons, billions of years long; the shortest are Chrons, a few thousand years long. In between come Eras, Periods, Epochs and Ages.

- **Fossil time**
  Because different plants and animals lived at different times in the Earth's past, geologists can tell how long ago rocks formed from the fossils in them. Using fossils, they have divided the Earth's history since Precambrian times into 11 Periods.

- **Geological column**
  Layers of rock form one on top of the other, so the oldest is usually at the bottom, unless they have been disturbed. The sequence of layers from top to bottom is called the geological column.

FACTS: About dating

- **Fossil dating**
  By looking for certain key fossils, geologists can tell whether one layer of rock is older than another so they can then place it within the geological column. This is called 'biostratigraphy'.

- **Absolute date**
  Fossils can show only if a rock is older or younger, not give a date in years — and many rocks don't contain fossils. To give an 'absolute' date, geologists often use radioactivity.

- **Radioactive dating**
  After certain substances such as uranium and rubidium form, their atoms slowly break down into different atoms, sending out rays as they do so. The rays are called radioactivity. By assessing how many atoms in a rock have changed, geologists can tell how old it is.

Precambrian time: The first lifeforms (bacteria) appear, and give the air oxygen

Cambrian Period: No life on land, but shellfish flourish in the oceans

Ordovician Period: Early fish-like vertebrates appear. The Sahara is glaciated

Silurian Period: First land plants. Fish with jaws and freshwater fish

Devonian Period: First insects and amphibians. Ferns and mosses as big as trees

Carboniferous Period: Vast warm swamps of fern forests which form coal. First reptiles

Permian Period: Conifers replace ferns as big trees. Deserts widespread

Triassic Period: First mammals. Seed-bearing plants spread. Europe in the tropics

Jurassic Period: Dinosaurs widespread. Archaeopteryx, earliest known bird

Cretaceous Period: First flowering plants. The dinosaurs die out

Tertiary Period: First large mammals. Birds flourish. Widespread grasslands

Quaternary Period: Many mammals die out in Ice Ages. Humans evolve

Proterozoic 2,500–590 m.y.a.

Precambrian

590 m.y.a.

Cambrian Period

505 m.y.a.

438 m.y.a.

408 m.y.a.

360 m.y.a.

Ordovician Period

Silurian Period

Devonian Period

Carboniferous Period

286 m.y.a.

Palaeozoic Era

Permian Period

248 m.y.a.

Triassic Period

213 m.y.a.

Jurassic Period

144 m.y.a.

Mesozoic Era

Cretaceous Period

65 m.y.a.

Tertiary Period

Cenozoic Era

Quaternary Period

2 m.y.a.

Today

Key to lifeforms
1. Jellyfish
2. Trilobite
3. Acanthodian (jawed fish)
4. Cooksonia (early land plant)
5 Ichthyostega (early amphibian)
6. Dimetrodon (early mammal-like reptile)
7. Anteosaurus
8. Herrerasaurus (early dinosaur).
9. Pterandon (early flying reptile)
10. Cephalopod (squid-like shellfish)
11. Brachiosaurus (dinosaur)
12. Crusafontia (small mammal)
13. Merychippus (early horse)
14. Proconsul (great ape)
15. Homo sapiens (early man)

159

Rocks

ROCKS ARE THE HARD MASS the ground is made of. You can only see bare rock exposed on the surface in a few places – cliffs, mountain crags and quarries. But it is there everywhere, not far beneath the city streets or the thin covering of soil or vegetation. Some rocks are just a few million years old; some are almost as old as the Earth. But they all tend to be very tough solids made of tiny crystals or 'grains' of naturally occurring chemicals called minerals. All these minerals came originally from the Earth's hot interior, but at the surface they form three kinds of rock: igneous, sedimentary and metamorphic.

FACTS: About igneous, sedimentary and metamorphic rock

▲ 90 per cent of the Earth's crust is made from igneous rocks, like this granite, which is an intrusive rock and formed underground.

▲ Although most surface rock is igneous, 75 per cent of the world's land surface is covered by thin layers of sedimentary rock like this limestone.

▲ Metamorphic rock such as this hornfels is rock made when other rock is altered by extreme heat or pressure.

- **Igneous rock**
  Igneous rock is formed from red hot magma (molten rock) that wells up from the Earth's interior. Some erupts on the surface through volcanoes and cools to form 'volcanic' or 'extrusive' igneous rock. Some is pushed up under the surface, forming 'intrusive' igneous rock.

- **Acid and basic igneous rock**
  There are many different kinds of rock. Some, like granite, are generally light in colour and are made from quite acidic magma (rich in silica). Others, like basalt, are darker and made from basic magma.

- **Sedimentary rock**
  Sedimentary rock forms in thin layers from debris that settles mainly on the seabed and is then squeezed and cemented over millions of years into solid rocks. Some, like limestone, are made mainly from plant and animal remains. Most are made from fragments of rock worn away by the weather.

- **Metamorphic rock**
  Metamorphic rock is made when other rocks are crushed by movements of the Earth's crust or scorched by magma — and changed so much that they form a new kind of rock, such as marble or slate.

FACTS: About coal and oil

In the Carboniferous Period, there were huge tropical swamps filled with giant, tree-like ferns. It is these that most coal formed from, as the remains of the plants were buried and squeezed.

1. Remains of swamp plants were first buried and squeezed to make peat

2. As they became buried deeper, heat and pressure changed the peat to brown coal

3. Further pressure changed brown coal to black bituminous coal and finally anthracite

- **Fossil fuels**
  Coal, oil and natural gas are fossil fuels, which means they formed over millions of years from the remains of plants and small creatures.

- **Carboniferous swamps**
  Most coal formed from the remains of plants that grew in huge, warm swamps in the Carboniferous Period, 300 million years ago.

- **Oil-bearing rocks**
  Oil formed from the remains of tiny plants and animals that lived in warm seas. As they died, they were buried and squeezed into oil, then collected in porous (sponge-like) layers of rock.

- **Crude oil**
  Oil usually comes up from the ground as thick, black 'crude' oil and must be refined for use.

The materials rocks are made of is continually recycled to make new rocks in a process called the rock cycle. Magma from the interior cools to form igneous rock which is gradually worn away by the weather. The fragments are washed down into the sea and settle on the seabed to form sedimentary rock. Both sedimentary and igneous rock may be altered into metamorphic rock — and all three are eventually broken down so that they too can be formed into new sedimentary rocks.

1. Igneous rocks form from magma forced up from the Earth's interior

2. Weather wears away the rock and fragments are washed into the sea, then settle on the seabed

3. Sediments buried under the seabed are cemented into layers of rock, then lifted up above the sea to be worn away again

Minerals

MINERALS ARE THE natural chemicals from which the Earth's crust is made. A few are powdery or resinous, but most are crystals. Usually, minerals occur as a mass of tiny crystals or grains. Occasionally, though, crystals grow as big as flagpoles. Geologists identify minerals by various factors including the colour and shape of the crystal. There are 2,000 or so different minerals, but fewer than 100 are common. A handful of minerals are pure chemical elements that occur naturally, such as gold or silver. Most are compounds, of which by far the most common are silicates.

FACTS: Gems

- **Gems**
  Gems are especially rare and beautiful mineral crystals such as rubies and emeralds.

- **Veins and geodes**
  Many precious gems form either in veins, where hot volcanic fluid forces its way into a crack in the rock, or in gas pockets in cooling volcanic rock called geodes.

  ▲ *Gems are rare because they only form naturally under very special conditions — usually deep within volcanic rocks. A few can now be made artificially, but these are not so precious.*

- **Diamonds**
  Diamonds are very hard, very rare — and very old. They were probably made by the mighty collision of continents during subduction (see page 157) and taken deep into the Earth. They are found only because volcanoes bring them near the surface again after billions of years.

- **Coloured gems**
  Many gems get their vivid colours from tiny traces of chemicals within them. Traces of iron turn common clear quartz into purple amethyst. Manganese turns quartz pink.

FACTS: About crystals

- **What are crystals**
  Crystals are glassy-looking, brittle solids that form in regular shapes, with sharp corners and flat sides.

- **Crystal shapes**
  Crystals are regular and there are only a certain number of possible basic regular shapes, called systems — cubic, pyramid and so on. The crystals of each mineral fit into one of these systems.

▶ *Minerals only rarely form in large, distinct crystals like these. Most of the time they form much smaller grains, and are mixed in with other minerals in rocks. Granite, for instance, is made of the minerals feldspar, quartz and mica, along with small amounts of other minerals. Quartz is a silicate mineral — the most common silicate mineral of all — but over 99 per cent of it is actually mixed in with other minerals in granite and other rocks, such as sandstone.*

Twists of silver

Bismuth rarely occurs in pure form in nature. It is usually mixed with sulphur

Silver rarely looks silvery in nature because exposure to air tarnishes the surface black

FACTS: Elements & silicates

- **Native elements**
  Native elements are minerals that occur naturally as pure chemical elements, including all those shown on this page.

- **Silicates**
  Silicates are minerals that form when the chemical elements silicon and oxygen — two of the most common elements on the Earth — combine with a metal. There are over 500 of them, including quartz, olivine and pyroxene.

▼ *Gold is rare but almost always found in pure form because it just won't mix with any other mineral.*

Copper only rarely occurs in pure form. Normally it is linked into minerals such as chalcopyrite

Yellow crystals of sulphur are often found around the smoking vents of volcanoes

Yellow fluorite is a rare mineral made of calcium and fluorine

The green crystals are uraninite, chemically uranium oxide, the main source of the metal uranium

163

Volcanoes

VOLCANOES ARE PLACES where hot molten rock or 'magma' from the Earth's interior erupts on the surface. With some volcanoes, it oozes out gently and flows overground as lava – red hot liquid rock. Others get clogged up with thick plugs of magma and then suddenly burst through in a mighty explosion that sends up jets of steam and hurls scorching fragments of debris from under the plugs thousands of metres in the air. Most volcanoes occur near the cracks between the giant tectonic plates that make up the Earth's surface (page 157), but a few occur at 'hot spots' where plumes of hot magma rise under the crust.

FACTS: Types of volcanoes

- **Thick and thin magma**
  Volcanoes take many forms, but the most explosive volcanoes occur near subduction zones where the collision of tectonic plates creates a very thick, sticky 'acid' magma that clogs up the volcano easily. Where plates are pulling apart, the magma is less acid and runs freely.

- **Cinder volcanoes**
  Most volcanoes are made of solidified lava, but some are mounds of ash.

◀ When the lava is quite runny, it floods out far and wide, creating a broad, gently sloping 'shield' volcano.

◀ The thick lava from explosive volcanoes piles up steeply around the volcano, creating a cone.

◀ In 'strato' volcanoes, alternate layers of ash and lava build up as ash falls on the lava flow from each eruption.

▶ The biggest eruptions are powered by a combination of steam and bubbles of carbon dioxide gas. Extreme pressure normally keeps them dissolved in the magma, but as the eruption begins the pressure drops and bubbles begin to form in the magma and swell rapidly. The eruption sends out three kinds of material apart from steam and gas — clouds of ash, solid fragments of the volcanic plug called tephra or volcanic bombs, and lava. Sometimes, lethal clouds of glowing ash hurtle down the slope.

▼ It is very hard to tell exactly when a volcano is going to erupt. But vulcanologists can get an idea by keeping a very careful watch on the slopes of the volcano, using laser rangefinders for accuracy. Any very slight change in slope might be the magma bulging up underneath, indicating an imminent eruption.

Eruptions begin with a build-up in pressure in the 'magma chamber' beneath the volcano

▲ Water heated under pressure underground by hot magma can burst onto the surface in a ferocious jet of steam and hot water called a geyser. The biggest geysers are hundreds of metres high.

Big eruptions can send so much ash into the upper air that they blot out the sun and turn the world cool

Tephra vary in size from tiny 'lapilli' to volcanic 'bombs', which can measure up to 1m across

Lava flows look spectacular, but it is ash which is really deadly

FACTS: Famous eruptions

▲ The eruption of Mt St Helens in Washington, USA, in 1980 was one of the biggest to rock North America this century. The eruption blew away the top of the mountain and blanketed the forest far around with ash.

- **Big bang**
  The eruption of Krakatoa, east of Java, in 1883 was so loud that people heard it in America.

- **Grey skies**
  The eruption of Mt Tambora in Java in 1815 sent up so much dust that the sun was blocked out right round the globe, causing two years of poor summers.

- **Roman remains**
  When Mt Vesuvius in Italy erupted in AD79, the people of the Roman town of Pompeii were buried instantly. The remains of the city, almost perfectly preserved under the ash, were discovered in the 18th century.

- **Biggest in human history**
  There was a giant eruption 20,000 years ago of Sumatra's Mt Toba, which covered the entire island in ash 300m deep.

- **Biggest ever**
  One of the biggest-ever eruptions covered nearly all of India in lava 65 million years ago.

Earthquakes

 EVEN A PASSING LORRY can make the ground tremble, but most earthquakes are the ground shuddering as the huge tectonic plates that make up the Earth's surface (see page 157) grind past each other. Most of the time the plates slide past each other quietly. But they sometimes jam. Then pressure builds up until they suddenly lurch on again, sending shock waves radiating in all directions. The nearer a place is to where the earthquake began – called the epicentre on the surface – the more severe the earthquake is. The worst earthquakes can bring down mountains and destroy cities.

FACTS: Earthquake zones

▲ Earthquake zones — places which suffer earthquakes repeatedly — are near plate edges, such as SE Europe and the Pacific coast.

- **San Andreas**
  The San Andreas fault in California is where two great plates slide past each other, often setting off earthquakes, such as that which destroyed San Francisco in 1906.

- **Predicting earthquakes**
  Earthquakes are hard to predict, but they are most likely to occur in earthquake zones — especially when there has not been one for some time. Seismologists use satellites and laser beams to detect slight movements, and look for changes in the magnetism of rocks.

DATA: The worst earthquakes

- **856**: 200,000 people killed in Damghan, Iran.
- **1138**: 230,000 people killed in Aleppo, Syria.
- **1556**: 830,000 people killed in Shansi, China.
- **1737**: 300,000 people killed in Calcutta, India.
- **1908**: 100,000 people killed in Messina, Italy.
- **1920**: 200,000 people killed in Gansu, China.
- **1923**: 144,000 people killed in Kwanto, Japan.
- **1976**: 255,000 people killed in Tangshan, China.
- **1995**: The earthquake in Kobe, Japan, killed 5,200 people, destroyed 190,000 buildings and left 300,000 people homeless.
- **1999**: 40,000 people killed in northwestern Turkey.
- **2004**: 225,000 people killed in 12 Asian countries.
- **2005**: 80,000 people killed in Pakistan.

Raised freeways are very vulnerable to earthquake damage

FACTS: About earthquake measurement

▲ *Seismometers detect tremors in the ground and display them on a seismograph. The strong vibrations of big earthquakes show as dramatic zig-zags.*

- **Richter scale**
  The severity of an earthquake, measured on a machine called a seismometer, is usually assessed on the Richter scale, which goes from 1 (slight tremor) to over 9 (severe earthquake).

- **Mercalli scale**
  The Richter scale gives the absolute magnitude (size) of an earthquake, but no idea of its effects. These are sometimes assessed on the Mercalli scale, which rates the damage done on a scale of 1 (barely noticeable) to 12 (total destruction).

Earthquakes usually last only a few minutes, but their effects can be devastating

Tall buildings are especially prone to earthquake damage

▼ *This picture shows the destruction that occurs when buildings lie directly over a fault in the Earth's crust. But the shock waves — called seismic waves — can be devastating even tens of kilometres from the epicentre. A great deal of damage is done by an earthquake itself, as the tremors shake buildings to pieces and snap roadways. But they can also fracture gas pipes and electricity cables and set off terrible fires.*

This earthquake is set off by the two edges of a fault sliding past each other

Mountains

MOUNTAINS LOOK FAIRLY PERMANENT but they are continually being created and destroyed. Most of the biggest mountains are actually quite young in geological terms. The Himalayas of Asia, for instance, include the world's highest peaks, yet they were first raised less than 40 million years ago – and they are still growing today. Mountains are created in one of a number of ways. Most are created by the folding of rock layers as the huge tectonic plates that make up the Earth's surface crunch together. Others are created as crustal movements lift up huge blocks. Others are created by volcanic eruptions.

FACTS: About fold mountains

- **Fold ranges**
  Most of the world's greatest mountain ranges — the Himalayas, the Andes, the Rockies, the Caucasus and the Alps — are created by the crumpling edges of colliding tectonic plates. This is why they often form long narrow ranges along the edges of continents. The Himalayas were created by the collision of India with Asia.

- **Runny mountains**
  The rock in mountains is not completely rigid. It flows a bit like very stiff treacle. So ranges such as the Himalayas are flowing out and getting flatter at the edges, at the same time as they are being pushed up.

- **Dip and strike**
  The angle at which folded rock layers are tilted is the 'dip'. This can be anything from a few degrees to over 90°. The direction of the fold is the 'strike'.

- **Upfold and downfold**
  Downfolds (like a dish) are called synclines; upfolds (like an arch) are called anticlines.

- **Overturned folds**
  Sometimes a fold may fold right over. This is called an 'overturned' fold. If it folds so far that it rests on the next fold it is said to be 'recumbent'.

▲ *If tectonic plates go on pushing together, the folding may go well beyond a simple fold (top). First it overturns and the layers begin to snap (middle). Finally the layers snap altogether, creating a 'nappe'.*

The Alps were created by folding, but the dramatic shape of the Matterhorn, one of the highest Alpine peaks (over 4,000m high), was created by glaciers.

DATA: The highest mountains

- Everest in the Himalayas is the world's highest (8,848m).
- South America's highest is Aconcagua (6,960m).
- North America's highest is Mt McKinley (6,194m).
- Africa's highest is Kilimanjaro (5,895m).
- Europe's highest is El'brus in Russia (5,642m).
- Australasia's highest is Papua New Guinea's Mt Wilhelm (4,884m).

FACTS: Faults & blocks

▶ As the tectonic plates of the Earth's crust jostle together, they may put rocks under such strain that they fracture, creating cracks or 'faults' in the rock. Large blocks of rock may then be thrown up to create mountains.

A fault scarp is a cliff, exposed as a massive block of rock is thrown up or down

- **Where faults occur**
  Faults occur mainly in areas that are called 'fault zones'. These lie mostly along the edges of tectonic plates.

- **Normal fault**
  In most faults, the cracking of the Earth's crust as tectonic plates pull apart allows a block of rock to slip straight down. In a 'wrench' fault, however, blocks slip sideways past each other. In a 'reverse' fault, one block slides up over another as plates crunch together.

- **Horsts and rifts**
  If a block of rock is thrown down between two faults it may create a deep, steep-sided 'rift' valley. If the block is thrown upwards, it creates a high plateau called a horst.

▼ No mountain range lasts forever. Sooner or later they are worn down by the weather. Frost, for instance, may shatter rocks on mountain peaks, leaving the lower slopes littered with fragments known as scree.

Rivers

RIVERS RUN DOWN to the sea or lakes wherever there is enough rain or melting snow to keep them flowing. Even when it is not raining, most rivers in moist regions are kept flowing by water from underground. This is because a lot of rain does not flow directly over the land, but seeps into the ground – only to bubble up lower down, in places called springs. Most rivers are very tiny as they start high up in the hills, tumbling over rocks and rapids. But they get bigger further down as they are joined by tributaries (side rivers). As they near the sea, they run in broad, smooth-flowing curves called meanders.

Heavy rainfall and melting snow high up starts a river with plenty of water

High up, the river tumbles over rocks and rapids in steep, narrow valleys

FACTS: About river valleys

◄ The Grand Canyon in the USA is one of the world's deepest river valleys, carved by the Colorado river over millions of years. The area is so dry that there is little rain to wear away the valley sides so these sides are often steep cliffs.

• River power
Rivers continually batter their banks and beds with running water, sand and pebbles. Over thousands of years, rivers can carve huge valleys out of solid rock.

• Valley to plain
To start with, river valleys are narrow, steep-sided and winding — and they are usually like this near their source in the hills. But, with time, they carve out broader, flatter valleys, and they meander over a wide 'floodplain' — a flat area liable to flooding when heavy rain or melting snow makes the river full.

▲ *Every river has a natural tendency to wind — especially in the lower reaches, where it is wide and deep and flows across a broad plain. Here, giant horseshoe-shaped meanders develop as the river wears away the outside bank of each curve and washes up sediment on the inside.*

In the lower reaches, the river is broad and deep and flows through smooth channels of sediment, washed down from higher up

Where it meets the sea, the river may split into several branches, forming a 'delta'

▲ *A river changes dramatically in character as it runs down towards the sea. High up, it is a small stream, tumbling over rocks because it is too small to wash them out of the way. Near the sea it flows through a smooth channel of silt and mud washed down by the river from higher up, over tens of thousands of years.*

FACTS: About waterfalls

- **Where falls form**
  Waterfalls typically form where a river flows over a band of hard rock, as the water wears away the soft rock below.

- **'The smoke that thunders'**
  So much water flows over Victoria Falls in Zimbabwe — 935 cubic metres every second — that the roar can be heard over 40km away.

▼ *The Angel Falls in Venezuela — named after an American pilot, Jimmy Angel — is the highest waterfall in the world, plunging 979m.*

DATA: The longest rivers

- The Nile in Africa is 6,673km long.
- The Amazon in S. America is 6,570km long.
- The Yangtze in Asia is 6,276km long.
- The Mississippi-Missouri in N. America is 6,019km long.
- The Danube in Europe is 2,857km long.

171

Oceans

ALMOST THREE-QUARTERS of the world is under water. There are five great oceans – the Pacific, the Atlantic and Indian – which all merge into the Southern Ocean around Antarctica – and the smaller Arctic Ocean. Then there are many smaller stretches of water called seas, including the Mediterranean, the Baltic and the Red seas. Yet, until quite recently, the bottom of the oceans was as mysterious and unknown as the surface of Mars. Modern ocean surveys have now begun to reveal that the landscape of the ocean bed is as varied as that of the continents, with high mountains, vast plains and deep valleys.

FACTS: About coasts

- **Eroded coasts**
  In some places, especially on headlands, coasts are worn away by waves crashing on bare rock. Hills are cut back to sheer cliffs, leaving behind platforms of rock washed over by the waves and, occasionally, isolated stacks of rock.

- **Sandy coasts**
  In other places, especially bays, material worn away is deposited as sandy and pebbly beaches and bars across river mouths.

- **Tides**
  In most places, the sea rises then falls back again twice daily. These 'tides' are created by the pull of the Moon's gravity which creates a tidal bulge of raised water on opposite sides of the world. As the Earth turns beneath the Moon during the day, so the tidal bulge moves around the world.

▼ *Constant battering by waves and salty water gives coastlines their own unique range of landforms, including cliffs, headlands and sandy bays.*

Beach

Crustose lichen

Sand bar

Estuary

Stack

Groyne to stop sand being washed along the beach

Headland

FACTS: About the ocean bed

- **Ocean floor revealed**
  In the last 30 years, surveys using sound equipment and robot submarines have allowed oceanographers to lift away the ocean waters to create detailed maps of the ocean floor (right).

- **Shallow margin**
  Around the edge of each ocean is a shelf of shallow water called the continental shelf. At the edge of this shelf, the ocean floor plunges to the deep ocean floor or 'abyssal plain'.

- **Seamounts**
  The abyssal plain is not completely flat but dotted, especially in the Pacific, with huge mountains known as seamounts, often thousands of metres high. In places, there are flat-topped seamounts called guyots, which may once have projected above the surface and been worn flat there.

◄ *In this map of the ocean floor, the light blue is the continental shelf, the dark blue is the abyssal plain.*

▲ *Sonar systems map the ocean floor by sending out high-frequency pulses of sound. The time it takes for the sound pulse to echo back from the ocean floor indicates how deep the ocean is.*

DATA: The oceans

- **SEA AREA**
  The seas cover more than 361 million square km of the Earth's surface. The biggest ocean is the Pacific, over 165 million square km, more than a third of the Earth's surface.

- **WATER VOLUME**
  There is 1.35 billion cubic km of water in the oceans.

- **DEEP WATER**
  The average depth of the oceans is 3,730m – enough to drown most Alpine mountains.

- **DEEPEST WATER**
  The deepest point on the Earth's surface is the Challenger Deep in the Marianas trench in the west Pacific, which is 10,920m deep.

173

Key facts: Planet Earth

Highest waterfalls

Angel Falls (Venezuela) 979m
Yosemite Falls (USA) 739m

Mardalsfossen (S)(Norway)	739m
Tugela Falls (S. Africa)	613m
Cuquenan Falls (Venez.)	610m
Sutherland Falls (NZ)	580m
Ribbon Falls (USA)	491m
Great Falls (Guyana)	488m
Mardalsfossen (N)	468m
Della Falls (Canada)	440m
Gavarnie Falls (France)	422m
Skjeggedal Falls (N'way)	420m
Glass Falls (Brazil)	404m
Krimml Falls (Austria)	400m
Trummelbach Falls (Switz)	400m
Takakkaw Falls (Canada)	366m
Silver Strand Falls (USA)	357m
Wallaman Falls (Aus)	347m
Wollomombi Falls (Australia)	335m

Cities

The world's biggest cities

São Paulo	18,628,000
Mexico City	18,268,000
Calcutta	13,217,000
Delhi	12,791,000
Tokyo	12,310,000
Jakarta	12,300,000
Bombay	11,914,000
Rio de Janeiro	11,227,000
Cairo	10,834,000
Dhaka	10,403,000
Seoul	10,281,000
Istanbul	10,243,000
Moscow	10,101,000
Shanghai	10,031,000
Paris	9,644,000
Karachi	9,269,000
New York	8,086,000
London	7,172,000

Continents

Asia
Area 44,380,400 sq km
Population 3,868,000,000
Population density
(People per sq km) 203

Africa
Area 30,313,000 sq km
Population 874,000,000
Population density 65

Antarctica
Area 14,000,000 sq km

North America
Area 24,211,000 sq km
Population 470,000,000
Population density 32

South America
Area 17,833,000 sq km
Population 350,000,000
Population density 49

Europe
Area 10,493,000 sq km
Population 729,000,000
Population density 175

Oceania
Area 8,510,000 sq m
Population 32,359,000
Population density 6

Population

The most populous countries

China	1,299,000,000
India	1,081,000,000
USA	293,850,000
Indonesia	222,611,000
Brazil	180,542,000
Pakistan	151,600,000
Russia	144,315,000
Bangladesh	135,255,000
Nigeria	128,254,000
Japan	127,757,000
Mexico	105,447,000
Philippines	82,670,000
Germany	82,561,000
Vietnam	81,839,000

Biggest lakes

Caspian Sea	370,963 sq km	Lake Ontario	18,999 sq km
Lake Superior	84,236 sq km	Lake Balkhash	18,426 sq km
Lake Victoria	69,458 sq km	Lake Ladoga	17,701 sq km
Aral Sea	64,496 sq km	Lake Chad	16,316 sq km
Lake Huron	63,090 sq km	Lake Maracaibo	13,260 sq km
Lake Michigan	57,752 sq km	Patos	10,152 sq km
Lake Tanganyika	32,761 sq km	Lake Onega	9,608 sq km
Lake Baikal	31,492 sq km	Lake Eyre	9,318 sq km
Great Bear Lake	31,324 sq km	Lake Titicaca	8,287 sq km
Lake Nyasa	28,876 sq km	Lake Nicaragua	8,028 sq km
Great Slave Lake	28,565 sq km	Lake Mai-Ndombe	8,028 sq km
Lake Erie	25,810 sq km	Lake Athabasca	7,933 sq km
Lake Winnipeg	24,386 sq km		

Richest and poorest

The world's richest countries		The world's poorest countries	
GNP per head in the 2000s		GNP per head in the 2000s	
	$US		$US
Luxembourg	42,930	Ethiopia	100
Switzerland	38,380	Congo, Dem. Rep	110
San Marino	34,330	Somalia	110
Bermuda	34,950	Burundi	120
Norway	33,470	Sierra Leone	130
Denmark	32,050	Guinea-Bissau	160
Japan	32,030	Malawi	180
USA	31,910	Niger	190
Iceland	29,540	Eritrea	200
Finland	27,730	Chad	210
Sweden	26,750	Mozambique	220
Germany	26,620	Nepal	220
Netherlands	25,140	Mali	240
France	24,170	Rwanda	250

Mountains

The world's highest mountains

Asia

Everest	8,848m
K2	8,611m
Kanchenjunga	8,598m

South America

Aconcagua	6,960m
Ojos del Salado	6,908m
Bonete	6,872m

North America

McKinley	6,194m
Logan	5,951m
Citlaltépetl	5,610m

Africa

Kilimanjaro	5,895m
Kenya	5,200m
Margherita Peak	5,109m

Europe

Elbrus	5,642m
Dykh Tau	5,203m
Shkara	5,201m

Oceania

Wilhelm	4,509m
Cook	3,754m
Tasman	3,497m

Key facts: Planet Earth

Major rivers of the world

Nile	6,673km	Amur-Shilka	4,416km	St Lawrence	3,058km
Amazon	6,570km	Lena	4,400km	Rio Grande	3,030km
Yangtze	6,276km	Congo	4,374km	Tunguska, Lower	2,995km
Mississippi-Missouri-		Mackenzie-Peace-		Indus	2,897km
Red Rock	6,019km	Finlay	4,241km	Danube	2,857km
Ob-Irtysh	5,411km	Mekong	4,180km	Salween	2,849km
Yenesei-Angara	4,989km	Missouri-Red Rock	4,125km	Brahmaputra	2,736km
Yellow	4,630km	Niger	4,100km	Euphrates	2,736km
		Plate-Parana	3,943km	Para-Tocantins	2,699km
		Mississippi	3,778km	Zambezi	2,575km
		Murray-Darling	3,751km	Nelson-	
		Missouri	3,725km	S.Saskatchewan-Bow	2,575km
		Volga	3,531km	Paraguay	2,549km
		Madeira	3,241km	Amu Darya	2,541km
		Purus	3,211km	Kolyma	2,513km
		São Fransisco	3,201km	Ganges	2,494km
		Yukon	3,185km	Ural	2,428km

Islands

The world's biggest islands

	sq km
Greenland	2,175,600
New Guinea	789,950
Borneo	751,100
Madagascar	587,041
Baffin (Canada)	507,451
Sumatra (Indonesia)	424,760
Honshu, Japan	227,415
Great Britain	218,078
Victoria, (Can)	217,290
Ellesmere (Can)	196,236
Sulawesi (Indo)	189,216
South Island (NZ)	151,215
Java (Indo)	126,501

Earthquake disasters

Date	Location	death toll	Date	Location	death toll
BC464	Sparta, Greece	20,000	1906	San Francisco, US	3,000
AD856	Corinth, Greece	45,000	1908	Messina, Italy	160,000
856	Damghan, Iran	200,000	1920	Kanshu, China	200,000
893	Ardabil, Iran	150,000	1923	Kwanto, Japan	144,000
1038	Chihli, China	100,000	1960	Southern Chile	5,700
1138	Aleppo, Syria	230,000	1964	Anchorage,	
1293	Kamekura,			Alaska	131
	Japan	30,000	1970	Ancash, Peru	66,000
1556	Shansi, China	800,000	1976	Tangshan,	
1667	Shemaka,			China	655,000
	the Caucasus	80,000	1985	Michoacán,	
1731	Peking, China	100,000		Mexico	9,500
1737	Calcutta, India	300,000	1994	Northridge, US	60
1755	Lisbon, Portugal	100,000	1995	Kobe, Japan	5,200

Sea deeps

The deepest sea trenches

	metres from sea level
Mariana	10,920
Tonga	10,800
Philippine	10,057
Kermadec	10,047
Izu-Ogasawara	9,780
Kuril	9,550
North New Hebrides	9,175
New Britain	8,940
Puerto Rico	8,605
Yap	8,527

Glaciers

The world's longest glaciers

Lambert-Fisher Ice Passage (Antarctica)	515km
Petermanns Glacier (Greenland)	200km
Hubbard Glacier (N. America)	128km
Siachen Glacier (Karakoram, Asia)	75km
Skeidarajokull (Iceland)	48km
Tasman (New Zealand)	29km
Aletsch Gletscher (European Alps)	24km

Oceans & seas

Oceans

Pacific	162,250 sq km
Atlantic	82,440 sq km
Indian	73,440 sq km
Arctic	14,090 sq km

Seas

South China	3,447 sq km
Caribbean	2,754 sq km
Mediterranean	2,505 sq km
Gulf of Mexico	1,544 sq km
Sea of Japan	1,007 sq km
East China	752 sq km
North	575 sq km
Black	461 sq km
Baltic	422 sq km

Weather

The world's sunniest place is the Eastern Sahara, with sunshine for over 90 per cent of all daylight hours.

The world's hottest place is Dallol, Ethiopia, with an average temperature of 34°C in the shade.

The world's driest place is the Atacama Desert in Chile, with an annual average of just 0.51mm of rain.

The world's coldest place is Vostok in Antarctica, where it averages -57.8°C.

The world's major deserts

	square kilometres
Patagonian	673,000
Rub al-Khali	647,500
Kalahari	582,800
Chihuahuan	450,000
Taklimakan	362,600
Kara Kum	350,000
Great Sandy	338,500
Great Victoria	338,500
Gibson	310,800
Thar	259,000
Atacama	181,300
Sonoran	181,300
Simpson	103,600
An Nafud	103,600
Mojave	38,900
Death Valley	7,800
Sahara	9,065,000
Arabian	2,330,000
Gobi	1,295,000
Namib	1,290

Quiz: Planet Earth

1. What were the first living things on Earth?

2. Exactly how many hours, minutes and seconds does it take the Earth to spin round once?

3. In which geological period did the first humans appear?

4. There were creatures on land long before there were any in the sea: true or false?

5. Coal is the fossilized remains of swamp plants: true or false?

6. How thick is the Earth's mantle - 300km or 3,000km?

7. What is the name of the highest mountain in North America?

8. Mt Everest is gaining height: true or false?

9. Which continent has no mountains over 5,000m high?

10. Which country in South America has the wettest place on Earth?

11. Which volcano erupted and buried the Ancient Roman town of Pompeii in Italy?

12. Vulcanologists try to predict eruptions by looking for a slight swelling in a volcano: true or false?

13. The severity of earthquakes is measured on the Richard scale: true or false?

14. What is the name of the fault that sets off earthquakes in California?

15. San Francisco burned to the ground in 1906: true or false?

16. What is the name of the world's longest river?

17. Where is the longest glacier in the world?

18. Which is the biggest desert in the world?

19. Tides are created by the pull of the Moon's gravity: true or false?

20. The 'abyssal plain' is the name given to which part of the ocean - the shallow edge or the deep ocean floor?

Answers:

1. Bacteria
2. 23 hours, 56 minutes and 4.09 seconds
3. The Quaternary period
4. False
5. True
6. 3,000km
7. Mt McKinley
8. True
9. Australasia
10. Colombia
11. Vesuvius
12. True
13. False - its the Richter scale
14. The San Andreas fault
15. True
16. The River Nile
17. Antarctica
18. The Sahara
19. True
20. The deep ocean floor

SCIENCE

Electricity

ELECTRICITY IS THE ENERGY that makes everything from toasters to tube trains work. It is also linked with magnetism. Together they form one of the basic forces that holds the universe together – electromagnetism. Electricity starts with atoms and tiny parts of each atom called electrons. Just as magnets are drawn together, so electrons are drawn to the centre of the atom. This attraction is called 'electric charge'. Electrons have a 'negative' charge; atomic centres a 'positive' one. It is the combined attraction of billions of tiny electrons to billions of tiny atom centres that creates electricity.

▶ Electricity is generated in power stations and sent across the country along big cables carried on towers called pylons, or along cables buried underground. The electricity is sent down these cables at very high voltage (high pressure) to make sure they reach their destination.

▲ If a coil of wire is wrapped around a bar of iron, switching on the current turns the bar into a very powerful magnet, called an electromagnet, or solenoid. The grey curves show lines of magnetic force.

FACTS: Electromagnetism

- **Making electricity**
  When a coil of electric wire is moved near a magnet — or a magnet is moved near a coil — the magnetism draws electrons through the wire, creating an electric current.

- **Power stations and generators**
  Power stations make electricity using generators. In generators, turbines (like fan blades) are turned by running water or by steam heated by burning oil or coal, or by nuclear energy. The turning of the turbines turns banks of electric coils round magnets.

- **Electric motors**
  Just as moving magnets create electricity, so an electric current can make a magnet move. In electric motors, an electric current is sent through a coil wrapped round a magnet. The surge of electricity through the coil makes the magnet turn.

◀ *Electric light bulbs rely on the fact that when an electric current reaches a restriction in a wire — called resistance — the wire gets hot. Inside a light bulb, there is a very thin wire called a filament which glows white hot when you switch the current on. The bulb is filled with a non-reactive gas, such as argon, to ensure the filament doesn't burn up.*

FACTS: Static electricity

▶ *Lightning is the release of the huge charge of static electricity made as raindrops bash together in a thundercloud.*

- **Static charge**
  Static electricity is what makes dry hair go frizzy when you comb it and a nylon jumper tingle if you pull it off too fast. It is called static because it doesn't move, like electricity in a circuit. It is made when surfaces rub together. Electrons rub off one surface and on to the other. The extra electrons give it a negative electric charge. This attracts surfaces which have lost electrons and so are positively charged.

FACTS: About electric currents

- **Currents and circuits**
  Electric currents can move through certain materials in a continuous flow. But for the current to flow, there must be a complete loop or circuit.

- **Free electrons**
  Electric currents work like a row of marbles — flicking one jolts marbles down the row. The marbles are 'free' electrons — electrons not attached to atoms.

- **Conductors**
  Materials that have many free electrons, such as copper, make good conductors of electricity.

▲ *Batteries use chemical reactions to create electricity. Each cell (part) has a positive and negative electrode. In a car battery, the electrodes are metal (usually lead) plates dipped in acid.*

▲ *Car batteries are called wet cell batteries. Torch and radio batteries are 'dry cells.' They often have electrodes of zinc and graphite (ground carbon).*

Magnetism

MAGNETISM IS THE INVISIBLE FORCE between magnetic materials such as iron and nickel. It affects only a certain area around each magnet, called its 'field'. It is strongest at the two ends, or 'poles', of the magnet, and gets steadily weaker further away. Magnetism sometimes attracts magnetic materials to each other; sometimes it repels them. Magnetism works in opposite ways at each of a magnet's poles, and whether two magnets snap together or spring apart depends on which poles meet. If the same poles of each magnet meet, they push each other away. If opposite poles meet, they pull together.

FACTS: About the Earth's magnetic field

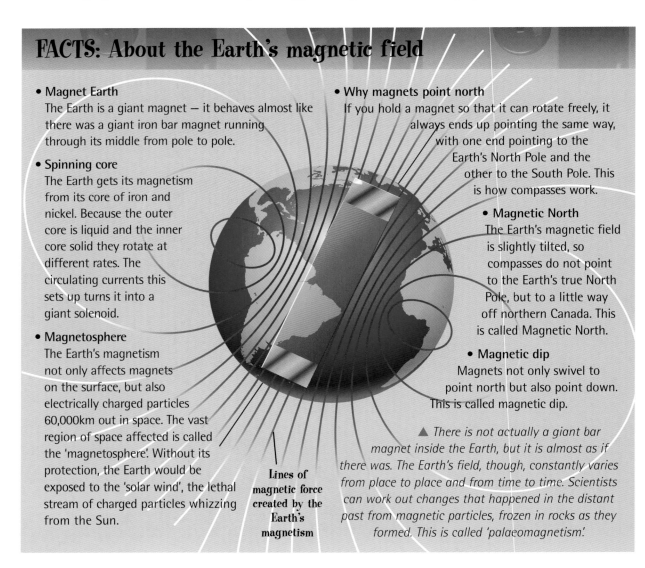

- **Magnet Earth**
  The Earth is a giant magnet — it behaves almost like there was a giant iron bar magnet running through its middle from pole to pole.

- **Spinning core**
  The Earth gets its magnetism from its core of iron and nickel. Because the outer core is liquid and the inner core solid they rotate at different rates. The circulating currents this sets up turns it into a giant solenoid.

- **Magnetosphere**
  The Earth's magnetism not only affects magnets on the surface, but also electrically charged particles 60,000km out in space. The vast region of space affected is called the 'magnetosphere'. Without its protection, the Earth would be exposed to the 'solar wind', the lethal stream of charged particles whizzing from the Sun.

- **Why magnets point north**
  If you hold a magnet so that it can rotate freely, it always ends up pointing the same way, with one end pointing to the Earth's North Pole and the other to the South Pole. This is how compasses work.

- **Magnetic North**
  The Earth's magnetic field is slightly tilted, so compasses do not point to the Earth's true North Pole, but to a little way off northern Canada. This is called Magnetic North.

- **Magnetic dip**
  Magnets not only swivel to point north but also point down. This is called magnetic dip.

Lines of magnetic force created by the Earth's magnetism

▲ There is not actually a giant bar magnet inside the Earth, but it is almost as if there was. The Earth's field, though, constantly varies from place to place and from time to time. Scientists can work out changes that happened in the distant past from magnetic particles, frozen in rocks as they formed. This is called 'palaeomagnetism'.

FACTS: Magnets

◀ *The effects of magnetic attraction are transmitted between objects affected by magnetism. So a magnet can pick up a string of paper clips.*

• **North and South Pole**
Every magnet has two ends: a north (north-seeking) pole and a south (south-seeking) Pole.

• **Magnetic domains**
Cut a magnet in half and you get two little magnets, each with north and south poles. You can go on dividing magnets into new magnets virtually down to atoms. This is because magnetic materials are made of tiny groups of atoms called domains, which are like mini-magnets.

• **Curie temperature**
Iron loses its magnetic properties above 760°C, called the Curie temperature after Pierre Curie, the scientist who discovered this.

▼ *Lines of magnetic force may be invisible, but they are real. Around a bar magnet, they form a hamburger shape. They crowd close together around the poles, where the field is strongest.*

▲ *Auroras are spectacular curtains of light that ripple through the night sky above the poles. The northern lights / Aurora Borealis are seen over the North Pole and the southern lights / Aurora Australis are over the South Pole. Auroras occur because there is a gaping hole in the Earth's magnetic field over the poles, where lines of magnetic force funnel in towards them. Every now and then, charged particles from the Sun stream in through the hole and cannon into air molecules at tremendous speed. The violent collisions make all the air molecules glow so brightly they light up the sky.*

▶ *The Ancient Chinese were probably the first to make magnetic compasses, for telling fortunes as well as finding directions. But sailors everywhere have been using compasses to navigate for more than a 1,000 years.*

185

Electronics

ELECTRONICS ARE AT THE HEART of a huge range of modern technologies, from hi-fis to rocket control systems. All work by using electricity to send signals. Inside every electronic device there are lots of small electric circuits continually switching on and off, telling the device what to do. But electronic switches are not like electric light switches on the wall; they work automatically. The most basic switches are 'transistors', which are made using special materials called semiconductors that change their ability to conduct electricity. Electronic systems work by linking lots of transistors together into 'integrated circuits', 'chips' and 'microprocessors'.

FACTS: About chips and microprocessors

- **Silicon chips**
  In most integrated circuits, dozens or even thousands of tiny transistors are joined together in circuits that are packed inside a single tiny slice of silicon. This is called a silicon chip.

- **Mini-chips**
  Chips are getting smaller and more sophisticated by the year. This is why even complex devices like powerful computers can be made pocket-sized.

- **Computer chips**
  The most complicated silicon chips are 'microprocessors' containing a million or more transistors. These are the brains in computers.

▲ The biggest things in a silicon chip are not all its circuits and switches — the tiny patch in the centre. The connectors that send its instructions to the rest of the machine — the teeth along the side of the chip — are much bigger.

▶ Televisions work by controlling a beam electronically. Inside is a 'gun' that fires a non-stop stream of electrically charged particles at the screen. Where it hits, it makes the screen glow by heating up its coating of phosphor. The picture is made of thousands of these glowing spots. Electronics control just where the gun hits the screen, make it glow and so create the picture.

Each gun hits the right colour dot – blue, red, green – and makes it glow

Colours are made with three guns – one for blue, one for green and one for red

A mask with small holes ensures each gun can hit only the right colour dot on the screen

FACTS: About computers

- **Binary code**
  Computers work electronically. Since electronic circuits can be only on or off, computers work by using a 'binary' system. This codes all data as strings of 1's or 0's — ons or offs.

- **Bits and bytes**
  Each 1 or 0 in a computer is called a 'bit' and bits are grouped together into bytes. This is why a computer's memory is measured in bytes. A kilo byte is 1,000 bytes. A megabyte is 1,000,000 bytes.

- **RAM and ROM**
  Some of a computer's memory, called the ROM (read-only memory) is built into its microchips. The RAM (random-access memory) takes new data and instructions whenever needed. Data can also be stored on magnetic patterns on removable discs, or on the laser-guided bumps on a CD.

▲ Many of the world's billions of computers are now linked down phone lines via the Internet, a system which controls all the links.

▼ Inside a computer are a number of microchips. At the heart is the central processing unit (CPU). The CPU is what works things out, within guidelines set by the ROM, and processes and controls all the programmes by sending data to the right place in the RAM.

▶ Computers are often controlled by a 'mouse'. Inside the mouse is a ball which turns as the operator glides the mouse over the table. The movement of the ball moves a pointer, or 'cursor', on the screen.

RAM   **CPU (inside) where all data is processed**   **Slot for disc drive**   **Power transformer**

Solar panels provide electric power for both electronic devices and motorized tasks, such as adjusting stabilizers

▶ Satellite and space technology depends on the sophisticated and compact control provided by electronic systems. Every spacecraft has its own onboard computers, and electronic circuits allow probes to be guided through elaborate tasks over millions of miles of space.

Radiation

RADIATION IS BASICALLY energy shot out by atoms at very high speeds. Some kinds of radiation are tiny particles splitting off from the atom. This is called radioactivity. But most radiation is tiny bursts of vibration or 'waves' such as X-rays, microwaves, radio waves and light. Light is the only form of radiation you can see; all the rest are invisible. Radiation that comes in waves is called electromagnetic radiation because it is linked to electricity and magnetism. But the length of the waves varies. The waves in gamma rays are very short, but they pack in a lot of energy, which is why they can be dangerous. Radio waves are very long and low in energy, which is why they are used for radio broadcasts. The rest come in between.

FACTS: About radioactivity and nuclear energy

Neutron

The splitting of uranium nuclei releases heat plus neutrons

Uranium nuclei

The splitting of nuclei releases neutrons which split more nuclei

▲ Nuclear fission relies on a chain reaction between atomic nuclei. Tiny alpha particles called neutrons are fired at uranium nuclei, splitting them. This not only creates heat but sets free more neutrons which shoot away and split up more uranium nuclei, releasing more neutrons which split more uranium nuclei and so on. Control rods in the power plant absorb neutrons and prevent the chain reaction getting out of hand.

• Radioactivity
Radioactivity is when an atom breaks down or 'decays', sending out radiation: lethal gamma rays (invisible electromagnetic waves) and two kinds of particle, 'alpha' particles and 'beta' particles.

• Nuclear radiation
Nuclear bombs and energy both create radioactive material. Radioactivity from bombs is huge, controlled and dangerous, causing death and radiation sickness and deforming unborn babies.

• Nuclear fission and fusion
In nuclear power stations, huge amounts of energy are released as heat from the nuclei of atoms by splitting them. This is called nuclear fission. Inside stars and in nuclear bombs, on the other hand, vast amounts of energy are unleashed when atomic nuclei are pushed together. This is called nuclear fusion.

▶ Nuclear bombs are the most devastatingly powerful bombs of all. They release so much energy so quickly that anything nearby is turned to dust which billows up in a huge mushroom-shaped cloud.

FACTS: Scans and X-rays

▼ *CT scans create a 3D picture of the inside of the body by making a complete circuit of the body along a particular 'slice' with X-rays. A computer then constructs the X-ray slices into a 3D picture.*

The patient is moved through the scanner as the X-ray gun rotates around her

◀ *SQUID scans pick up the tiny radiation from firing nerve cells, and so show the brain working in detail.*

• **X-rays**
X-rays can be picked up on photos just like light, even though we can't see them. They have enough energy to pass clean through skin, but are stopped by muscle and bone. So muscle and bone show up in silhouette on an X-ray photo, giving doctors a vital view inside the body to help reveal problems.

• **PET scans**
PET (Positron Emission Tomography) scans detect particles called positrons to show blood moving.

The waves are scattered around the oven by a fan

Microwaves are created by a device called a magnetron

▲ *Microwave cookers work by bombarding food with invisible microwaves. It is because they are electromagnetic that microwaves heat food so quickly. Molecules of water in the food are like magnets and they are turned to and fro so quickly by the electromagnetic vibrations that they get very hot very quickly.*

DATA: Radiation

• **SPEED**
All electromagnetic radiation moves at the speed of light, 300,000km per second.

• **RADIOACTIVE MATERIALS**
50 radioactive materials occur naturally, including uranium. 2,000, like plutonium, are made artificially.

• **HALF LIFE**
Half the atoms in a bit of strontium decay radioactively in just 9 mins. In uranium it takes 4.5 billion years.

Light

LIGHT IS JUST ONE OF THE FORMS of electromagnetic radiation, but it is vital to us. It is the only form we can see – and without it we could see nothing. Plants grow by soaking up light, too, and changing it into food. And light from the sun provides most of our warmth and energy. Yet, although we are surrounded by light during the day, very few things give out light. The Sun, the stars, electric lights and other things that glow are sources of light. But most things you see only because they reflect light from light sources. If they do not send out or reflect light, they are invisible like air.

FACTS: About reflection and refraction

- **See-through**
  When light rays hit something, they bounce off, are absorbed or pass through. Anything that lets light through like glass is 'transparent'. If it jumbles it on the way, like frosted glass, it is 'translucent'. If it stops light altogether it is 'opaque'.

- **Reflection**
  When light strikes a surface, some or all is reflected. From most surfaces it scatters in all directions. But from mirrors and shiny surfaces, it bounces off in the same pattern it arrived, giving a mirror image.

- **Refraction**
  When light goes into something transparent like glass or water, the rays are bent or 'refracted'. This happens because light travels slightly slower in glass or water.

◀ The refraction (bending) of light by water makes a straw in water look as if it is bent up in the middle. Of course, it is completely straight.

▲ When light is reflected off a mirror, it is reflected at just the same angle. The angle it hits, called the 'angle of incidence', is the same as the 'angle of reflection'.

▲ Glass lenses are shaped so that light is refracted in certain ways. Concave lenses (above) spread them out. Convex (below) lenses focus them (bring them together).

▲ Combinations of lenses in binoculars and telescopes gather light rays together to make things look bigger and closer.

FACTS: About light waves

▲ Most light contains a jumbled mixture of wavelengths. This is called 'incoherent' light. But in laser light, all the waves are the same length and travel in step. This is called 'coherent' light.

- **Light waves**
  Light travels in waves, like ripples on a pond. The waves are tiny — 2,000 would fit across a pinhead.

- **Light packets**
  A light beam is made up of millions of tiny packets of energy called photons.

- **Wavelength**
  Every photon has its own distinctive wavelength. The colour we see depends on the wavelengths of the photons.

- **Light from atoms**
  All light comes from atoms. When an atom is energized by, say, an electric spark or by heat, it becomes 'excited' and its electrons are moved. As they settle back to their normal position, they let fire a photon.

FACTS: About colour

- **Colour**
  When we see different colours, we are seeing different wavelengths of light. Light that contains an equal mix of all colours, like sunlight, appears white.

- **Red buses**
  The colours of objects depends on what wavelengths they soak up and what they reflect. A red bus is red because it soaks up every colour but red, and only bounces red back to your eyes.

- **Primary colours**
  You can make any colour of light by mixing red, green and blue light. You can make any colour of paint by mixing cyan (a bluish colour), magenta (a reddish colour) and yellow paint.

▲ Different colours are refracted different amounts. So white light splits into all the colours of the rainbow when it passes through a prism (a triangular block of glass).

Levers and machines

IN EVERY DAY LIFE we take advantage of all kinds of machines, from toasters to TVs. But, for a scientist, a machine is a device that makes life easier by reducing the effort needed to move something. There are always two forces involved in such a machine: a 'load', that is the force the machine is designed to overcome; and the 'effort', which is the force used to move the load. The amount a machine cuts the effort you need to move a load is called the 'mechanical advantage'. The mechanical advantage tells you how effective any machine is, whether it is a set of gears or a lever or a crane.

FACTS: About gears

- **How gears work**
  Gears can reduce work by spreading the Effort over a greater distance. This can make it easier to cycle uphill or for a car to accelerate from a standstill. They are pairs of wheels of different sizes that turn one another. They often have interlocking teeth to avoid slipping.

- **Gear ratio**
  The number of times the wheel that is driving turns the wheel that is driven is called the gear ratio. With a ratio of 5:1, the driving wheel turns five times for every time the driven wheel turns.

▶ *Inside a gear box, there are four or five pairs of gear wheels. Changing gear means selecting the right pair to make sure the best combination of speed and force is transmitted from the engine to the wheels.*

▼ *The pedal wheel and cogs on a bicycle wheel don't actually touch, but they are gears too, for the chain connects them just like the teeth on gear wheels.*

- **Increasing force**
  With a big gear ratio, the driven wheel turns slower relative to the driving wheel. But though it turns slowly, it turns with more force. This is why you select a big gear ratio to ride a bicycle uphill. Although you have to pedal much faster, pedalling is less effort.

- **Increasing speed**
  With a small gear ratio, the driven wheel turns with less force, but turns faster. This is why you select a smaller gear ratio for riding along a level road.

Some levers have the fulcrum between the load and the effort, like crowbars

Some levers have the load between the effort and the fulcrum, like wheelbarrows and screwdrivers

Some levers have the effort between the load and the fulcrum, like tweezers

▲ *A lever is a simple machine that makes it easier to move a load. If a rod is fixed at one point, but is free to swivel, it is a lever. The fixed point is called the fulcrum, and if you push on one end of the rod, your effort can be used to move a load on the other. This is called a turning effect. The further away from the fulcrum you apply your effort, and the nearer the load is, the more your efforts will be multiplied.*

FACTS: About machines

- **Spreading the load**
  Machines do not give anything for nothing. The amount of effort to move a particular load is always the same. They make a load easier to move by spreading the effort over a greater distance.

- **Velocity ratio**
  The distance moved by the effort you apply divided by the distance moved by the load is called the velocity ratio. If the velocity ratio is greater than 1, the effort moves further than the load. So you need less effort to move the load, but you have to apply it for longer.

- **Work**
  The sum of the efforts you put in to move something is called the 'work'. Work is basically the force you apply multiplied by the distance the load moves. Moving a load of 1kg over 10km always requires the same amount of work.

▼ *A mechanical digger uses powerful hydraulic (fluid-filled) systems to move its digging arms, but the same mechanical principles apply. The arms are levers and give the same mechanical advantage.*

Force and motion

A FORCE IS SIMPLY SOMETHING that pushes or pulls. Without forces, nothing in the universe would happen. Every object in the universe has its own 'inertia' – that is, it will not move unless it is forced to. So if something is moving, you can be sure it has been pushed or pulled. Similarly, once it is moving, it will go on moving forever, at the same rate and in the same direction, unless some force slows it down or speeds it up or pushes or pulls it off course. This is called 'momentum'. It is because heavy, fast moving objects have a great deal of momentum that car crashes do so much damage.

FACTS: About gravity

• **Universal pull**
Gravity is the force of attraction that holds us all on the ground and holds the universe together. In fact, every bit of matter in the universe has its own gravitational pull and attracts every other bit of matter. The strength of the pull depends on how massive things are and how far they are apart. Massive objects nearby exert a strong gravitational pull. Light objects far away exert little pull.

▼ *When you kick a football, at first the power of your kick overcomes air resistance and gravity and the ball climbs. But after a while, air resistance slows the ball, and gravity pulls the ball down to the ground. So it loops through the air.*

Gravity   Air resistance

At this point the pull of gravity exceeds the remaining force of the kick

If two balls are kicked together with equal force...

...they will bounce back with equal force

▶ *A tightrope walker can balance on the high wire when gravity pulls down equally on each side. This happens when the exact middle of his weight, called the 'centre of gravity', is directly over the wire.*

▶ *Space probes rely on gravity to pull them in towards planets. But, for a safe landing, they must slow down their descent with a parachute. But this only works for small planets; the gravitational pull of massive planets like Jupiter is too great for a parachute to have much effect.*

▶ When you measure the weight of an apple on a spring balance — or any other way — you are simply measuring the pull of gravity. The heavier the apple is — that is, the more mass it has — the more strongly it is pulled by the Earth's gravity, and so the further it stretches the spring on the spring balance which indicates its weight.

FACTS: Newton's Laws

▶ The great English scientist Isaac Newton (1642–1727) showed the link between force and motion in three Laws of Motion. He also discovered that the same force, gravity, made things fall and kept planets orbiting the Sun.

● **Mass and weight**
When an object is heavy, we talk of its weight. But scientists use the word 'mass'. Mass is how much matter it contains. They use weight only for the force of gravity — that is, how strongly an object pulls or is pulled by gravity.

● **Acceleration by gravity**
Like all forces, gravity makes things accelerate. So when things fall, they gain speed as they go down. On Earth they get faster at 9.8m per sec.

● **Terminal velocity**
As objects fall faster, the resistance of the air has more effect. Eventually, air resistance equals the pull of gravity and the object can fall no faster. It then falls at a steady speed. This speed is called the object's 'terminal velocity'.

● **Newton's First Law of Motion**
Newton's First Law is about how an object accelerates (or decelerates) only when a force is applied.

● **Newton's Second Law of Motion**
The Second Law is that the acceleration depends on the size of the force and the object's mass.

● **Newton's Third Law of Motion**
The Third Law is that when a force pushes or acts one way, an equal force pushes in the opposite direction.

● **Dynamics and statics**
The study of the way objects move when acted upon by forces is called dynamics. The study of things that do not move is called statics.

▼ Newton's laws work for every thing larger than an atom that moves in the universe, from an opening bud to a speeding truck.

Energy

FOR ANYTHING TO HAPPEN, for things to move or even change – for chocolate to melt or a rocket to fly – you need energy. Scientists say energy is 'the capacity to do work', and by this they simply mean energy makes things happen. It comes in many forms, from the chemical energy locked in sugar to the mechanical energy in a moving truck. But it always works in two ways: transfer or conversion. Energy transfer simply means it is moving from one place to another, like heat going up a chimney or a football being kicked. Energy conversion is when it changes from one form to another – from the steam-powered turbines to electric power in power stations, for instance.

FACTS: About solar energy

• **Solar power**
Energy that arrives as light from the Sun gives us virtually all our energy , either directly by its warmth or indirectly by, for instance, providing the energy to grow plants which are eventually converted into coal for burning.

• **Solar panels and cells**
Solar panels provide heat as water, sandwiched between sheets of glass, is heated by the Sun. Solar cells are light-sensitive chemicals which generate an electric current when hit by light.

▶ Each solar cell generates only a tiny electric current, but connecting hundreds together can create a significant amount of electricity.

▼ Honda's record-breaking experimental solar-powered car shows just what could be done with a car run entirely on sunlight.

▼ Less than half the energy from the Sun that strikes the Earth reaches the ground. 53% of it is absorbed or reflected on the way down through the atmosphere. 16% of this is soaked up by water vapour and dust in the air; 7% is scattered by the air; 3% is soaked up by clouds; 23% is reflected off clouds; and 4% is reflected by the land and oceans.

Almost a quarter of the sunlight reaching the Earth is reflected away off clouds

FACTS: Renewable energy

▲ *To build up water pressure to turn the turbines and to even the flow, most hydro-electric power stations are built inside big dams.*

- **Alternative energy**
  Fossil fuels are irreplaceable and pollute the air, so there is a search for clean, renewable alternatives, including electricity generated by winds, the sun (solar power), the tides or waves.

- **Hydro-electric power (HEP)**
  HEP is electricity generated by turbines turned by water. It is the only major alternative energy source.

FACTS: Energy sources

- **Fossil fuels**
  90 per cent of our energy comes from fossil fuels (page 161). About 40 per cent comes from oil, 27 per cent from coal and 21 per cent from natural gas. These sources are effectively non-renewable, since they took millions of years to make. So all the world's fossil fuels will eventually be used up.

- **Nuclear energy**
  Nuclear energy is also non-renewable but it uses fuel such as uranium so slowly that it will not run out in the near future. Unfortunately it leaves a dangerous radioactive waste.

▲ *When cars burn petrol, they not only use up a non-renewable source of energy, they also fill the air with polluting exhaust fumes such as nitrous oxides.*

Just 47% of sunlight is absorbed by the ground

◄ *Flowers and other plants get their energy directly from sunlight in a process called photosynthesis. This allows them to use carbon dioxide in the air to create the energy-rich chemical sugars they need for growth. Humans, like animals, have to get their energy indirectly, by eating plants — or by eating animals that have themselves eaten plants.*

Heat

HEAT IS NOT JUST THE WARMTH of the Sun or a fire; it is a form of energy, the energy of molecules moving. The faster molecules move, the hotter things are. When you feel the heat of a fire, you are simply being battered by millions of fast-moving air molecules – hurried up by millions of even faster-moving molecules in the fire. The fire heats the air because heat always spreads out, and something hot always makes its surroundings warm too as it itself loses heat and cools down. We measure how hot something is by its temperature. But temperature is just a measure of how fast the molecules are moving; heat is the total energy of all the moving molecules.

FACTS: About conduction, radiation and convection

- **Convection**
  Convection is when warm air rises through cool air, like a hot-air balloon. It rises because the warmth makes it expand and so it becomes less dense and lighter than the cooler air around.

  ◀ *Infra-red radiation from the intense heat caused by silicon crystal meltdown.*

  ▼ *The heat of a candle flame heats up a nearby thermometer mainly by radiation, which travels in waves, just like light.*

- **Spreading heat**
  Heat spreads in three ways: conduction, radiation and convection.

- **Conduction**
  Conduction is the spread of heat through substances by direct contact — a bit like a relay race, as vibrating molecules cannon into their neighbours and set them moving too. Good conducting materials like metals feel cool because they carry heat away quickly.

- **Radiation**
  Radiation is the spread of heat as heat rays — invisible 'infra-red' electromagnetic radiation (page 182). Radiation moves through space spreading heat without direct contact.

◀ Heat makes things expand. So thermometers can measure temperature by showing how much a liquid such as coloured alcohol expands and rises up a tube. Everyday temperatures are measured in degrees — Centigrade (°C) or Fahrenheit (°F). Water freezes at 0°C which is also 32°F. Water boils at 100°C (212°F). The temperature of the surface of the Sun is 6,000°C. Scientists, however, would say the Sun's temperature is 6,000K, because they use a scale called the Kelvin Scale which starts at -273°C.

FACTS: Pressure and heat

◀ If air is squeezed, it gets warmer as the pressure rises. You can see this for yourself if you pump up a bicycle tyre quickly. After a few pumps, it will feel quite warm. The pump works by squeezing air down through the tube with a plunger as you push down. On the upstroke, a one-way valve lets more air in.

- **What is pressure?**
  Pressure is the way water and air push against their surroundings. Molecules in air and water are always zooming about, and the pushing is actually all the molecules smashing into their surroundings.

- **Rising pressure**
  When air is squeezed, its pressure rises in proportion, because more molecules are squeezed into a smaller space. This is Boyle's Law.

- **Heat and pressure**
  If air cannot expand, heating it up boosts its pressure in proportion, because heat makes the molecules zoom about faster and smash harder into their surroundings. But, if it can expand, it swells in proportion instead. This is Charles's Law.

 # DATA: Temperatures

- **LOWEST TEMPERATURE**
  The lowest possible temperature is -273.15°C, when all molecules stop moving. This is called Absolute Zero. The lowest recorded on the Earth was -89°C.

- **HIGHEST TEMPERATURE**
  The highest temperature may be 20 million°C in the heart of stars. The highest on the Earth was 59°C.

Solids, liquids & gases

NEARLY EVERY SUBSTANCE IN THE UNIVERSE is either a solid, a liquid or a gas. These are said to be the three states of matter. They seem very different, but every substance can change from one to the other and back again, providing the temperature and pressure are right. Just as ice melts to water and water turns to steam when it gets hot, so every substance changes from solid to liquid to gas at certain temperatures. The temperature at which a substance melts from solid to liquid is called its melting point. The highest temperature a liquid can reach before turning to a gas is its boiling point.

FACTS: Three states of matter

Gas: water vapour

Liquid: rainwater

Solid: ice

◀ A gas, like air, does not have any shape, strength or fixed volume. This is because its molecules are moving fast enough to break the bonds that try to hold them together.

◀ A liquid flows and takes up the shape of any container it is poured into. This is because although bonds hold the molecules together, they are loose enough to fall over each other like dry sand.

◀ A solid has strength and a definite shape. This is because its molecules are bonded together firmly in a regular structure, and simply vibrate on the spot. The hotter it gets, the more they vibrate.

- **Melting**
  In a solid, molecules are held together tightly by bonds and simply vibrate on the spot. Heat makes them vibrate faster, until the bonds loosen. Eventually they become so loose that the neat structure breaks down, and the substance melts and flows all over the place.

- **Boiling**
  If the temperature goes on rising, the heat makes molecules zoom all over the place, until they move so fast that the molecules break away altogether. More and more molecules start shooting away from the surface as gas or steam. Eventually, all the liquid turns to gas.

◀ *The more firmly molecules are bonded together, the stronger and tougher solid they make. Diamond is the hardest solid of all, because all its molecules are bonded together in an incredibly strong structure.*

FACTS: About solutions

- **Special mixtures**
  Water often contains traces of other substances mixed in. If they're mixed so well that they are indistinguishable, the mixture is called a solution. Sea water is a solution of salts dissolved in water. Solutions play a vital part in our body chemistry.

- **Saturated solutions**
  When solids dissolve in a liquid, the solution becomes stronger and stronger until it becomes 'saturated' and no more dissolves. If it is heated, however, more will dissolve before it becomes saturated.

Stalactite

▶ *Some substances turn water acid — and acids are very good at dissolving things. Rain is a mild acid and can dissolve limestone rocks — then leave the minerals it dissolves as 'stalactites' in caves as it seeps through the ground.*

◀ *Sugar dissolved in tea is a solution. If you go on piling sugar in, it will eventually become saturated — as the sugar molecules fill the spaces between the water molecules.*

- **Evaporation**
  As a liquid heats up, more and more of its molecules break away from the surface, turning it to gas. This is called evaporation. When clothes dry, it is because water evaporates from them.

- **Condensation**
  When a gas cools, molecules slow down until bonds form between them, forming drops of liquid. This is called condensation. Water condensing from the air is called dew.

- **Ice, water and water vapour**
  Water is the only substance commonly found in all three states: solid ice, liquid water and gas. Water is called water vapour when it is a gas. Steam is actually lots of tiny drops of liquid water in air. Only when these drops evaporate does it turn to water vapour.

- **Space saving**
  Substances get smaller when they freeze as molecules pack tighter — except water. Water expands when it freezes, which is why ice bursts water pipes. It is also why ice floats, as it is less dense than water.

Stalagmite

Matter

MATTER IS EVERY SUBSTANCE in the universe, from the tiniest speck of dust to the largest star – everything that is not simply empty space. Surprisingly, though, even the most solid-looking matter is mostly empty space too, for matter is made from tiny pieces called atoms. You cannot see them, or the space between them, because they are amazingly small. You could fit 2 billion atoms on the full stop at the end of this sentence. Scientists once thought they were the smallest things in the universe – and that they were like tiny balls that could never be split or destroyed. But they are more like clouds of energy, and they too are mostly empty space, dotted with even tinier 'sub-atomic particles'.

FACTS: About atoms and sub-atomic particles

- **The atomic nucleus**
  The core of an atom is a cluster or 'nucleus' of two kinds of particle: protons and neutrons. Protons have a positive electrical charge. Neutrons have none.

- **Electrons**
  Whizzing round the nucleus as fast as the speed of light are even lighter particles called electrons. Electrons are negatively charged.

- **Atoms and ions**
  Most atoms have identical numbers of protons and electrons, so the electrical charges balance. An ion is an atom that has either lost or gained electrons, so it may be either positively or negatively charged.

- **Short-lived particles**
  By smashing atoms together at high speeds, scientists have found over 200 sub-atomic particles besides electrons, protons and neutrons, but most of these last only a fraction of a second.

- **Quarks and leptons**
  Scientists believe that all particles are made from just two basic kinds: quarks and leptons. Electrons are leptons. Protons and neutrons are made from different 'flavours' of quark.

◀ Protons are made from clusters of three quarks, held together by gluons. There are actually six different kinds of quark but only two — 'up' quarks and 'down' quarks — are long-lived, and this is what protons are made of.

▶ Atoms are not really like this. All the particles are really just clusters of energy that probably occur only in certain places. But it is a good way to imagine them, with electrons whizzing round the nucleus.

- **Atomic forces**
  Atoms can be split, but are usually held together by three forces — the electrical attraction between negative electrons and positive protons, and the 'strong' and 'weak' nuclear forces that bind together the particles of the nucleus. These forces, together with gravity, are the basic forces that hold the universe together.

FACTS: About crystals

- **Crystal shapes**
  Crystals are hard, shiny solids formed in regular geometric shapes. Grains of salt, sugar and sand are all crystals. So are diamonds. Each is made from a very regular structure of atoms, ions or molecules.

- **Crystallization**
  When melted substances turn solid or dissolved substances leave solutions, they form crystals. This is called crystallization.

- **Crystallography**
  Crystallography is the study of crystals, usually using X-rays (page 189).

▲ *Most hard substances are crystals. A powerful microscope reveals the regular structure of crystals of sulphur. The colours are computerized.*

Water molecule

◀ *Atoms rarely exist alone. Usually they join up in small groups called molecules. Hydrogen atoms, for instance, exist in pairs or joined to other atoms. A molecule of hydrogen gas is a pair of hydrogen atoms. A water molecule is a pair of hydrogen atoms joined to an oxygen atom.*

Nucleus of protons and atoms

Around the nucleus whirl clouds of tiny negatively charged electrons

▶ *The study of matter is called chemistry. In the past most chemistry was done in laboratories — boiling and mixing chemicals in flasks and test tubes. Now a great deal of chemistry is done on computer, constructing molecules in cyberspace. In this way chemists have been able to create entirely new chemicals.*

The elements

ALL THE SUBSTANCES IN THE UNIVERSE are made up from 100 or so basic chemicals or 'elements', such as gold and oxygen. Each element has its own unique character – and its own special atoms. Each element has a different number of protons and electrons in its atoms, from hydrogen with one of each to lawrencium with 103. The number of protons and electrons in their atoms is really the only difference between the elements, but this difference has a huge effect on their nature. Nitrogen gas atoms, for instance, have seven protons and carbon have six, just one less, but they are totally unlike.

FACTS: Groups and Periods

- **Rows and columns**
  The Periodic Table of elements is laid out in rows called Periods and columns called Groups.

- **Electron shells**
  Electrons spin round atoms in up to seven layers or 'shells'. There is a limit to how many electrons can fit in each shell. Only two fit in the first shell, closest to the nucleus, eight in the second and eight in the third. After that it gets complicated, but the outer shell never holds more than eight.

- **Shells and Periods**
  The number of electron shells an atom has increases down each Group. So every atom in each Period has the same number of electron shells. What varies is the number of electrons.

- **Electrons and Groups**
  Each Group is for elements with a certain number of electrons in their outer shells — and this is what determines an element's chemical properties. Every element in the same Group has similar properties.

- **Reactive to stable**
  Each Period starts on the left with a highly reactive 'alkali metal' which has one electron in its outer shell. It ends on the right with a stable 'noble gas', such as argon, which has eight electrons in its outer shell.

▼ All the elements can be displayed in order on a chart called the Periodic Table. The number of protons an element has in each of its atoms is called its atomic number, and the chart lists elements in atomic number order, starting with hydrogen at 1.

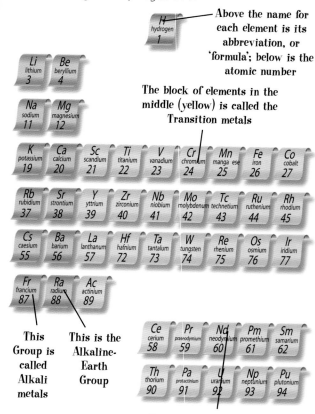

Above the name for each element is its abbreviation, or 'formula'; below is the atomic number

The block of elements in the middle (yellow) is called the Transition metals

This Group is called Alkali metals

This is the Alkaline-Earth Group

This row, called the lanthanides or rare earths, fits into Group 3

FACTS: About atomic mass and formulae

- **Atomic mass**
  Atomic mass is the 'weight' of an atom of an element and corresponds to the average number of protons and neutrons in the nucleus.

- **Formula**
  Every element has a short name, or formula. Carbon is C, Hydrogen is H, Copper Cu and so on.

▲ *Atoms of gold have 79 protons in their nuclei, and, on average, 118 neutrons. So its (relative) atomic mass is 197. The formula for gold is Au.*

These elements (purple) are called non-metals

As the Atomic Numbers increase by one along each period, so the chemical properties change

							He helium 2
	B boron 5	C carbon 6	N nitrogen 7	O oxygen 8	F fluo ine 9	Ne neon 10	
	Al aluminium 13	Si silicon 14	P phosphorus 15	S sulphur 16	Cl chlorine 17	Ar argon 18	

Ni nickel 28	Cu copper 29	Zn zinc 30	Ga gallium 31	Ge germanium 32	As arsenic 33	Se selenium 34	Br bromine 35	Kr krypton 36
Pd palladium 46	Ag silver 47	Cd cadmium 48	In indium 49	Sn tin 50	Sb antimony 51	Te tellurium 52	I iodine 53	Xe xenon 54
Pt platinum 78	Au gold 79	Hg mercury 80	Ti thalium 81	Pb lead 82	Bi bismuth 83	Po polonium 84	At astatine 85	Rn radon 86

These elements (blue) are called poor metals

The final Group on the right is the noble gases

Eu europium 63	Gd gadolinium 64	Tb terbium 65	Dy dysprosium 66	Ho holmium 67	Er erbium 68	Tm thulium 69	Yb ytterbium 70	Lu lutetium 71
Am americium 95	Cm curium 96	Bk berkelium 97	Cf californium 98	Es einsteinium 99	Fm fermium 100	Md mendelevium 101	No nobelium 102	Lr lawrencium 103

This row, called the actinides, fits into Group 3

FACTS: About metals

- **Metals**
  Metals are hard, dense, shiny solids. They conduct heat well. They are also good conductors of electricity because they are electropositive, which means electrons easily become 'free' (page 183).

- **Transition metals**
  Transition metals are metals in the midst of the Table like gold — shiny and tough, but easily shaped.

- **Lanthanides or rare earths**
  These silvery metals are called rare earths because they were once thought too reactive to stay in the ground unmixed with other elements for long.

FACTS: About noble gases

- **Nobly aloof**
  Group 0 is the far right group called the noble gases. The outer shells of their atoms are full up, so they do not react with other elements. They are sometimes called inert gases.

- **Bulb gases**
  Noble gases like argon and krypton are used in light bulbs because they are unreactive.

Chemicals and compounds

SOME SUBSTANCES, like gold, are made of just one element. Most are made of two or more elements joined together to make what is called a compound. Table salt, for instance, is a compound of the two elements sodium and chlorine. A compound is usually very different in nature from the two elements that make it up. Sodium, for instance, is a metal that fizzes and gets hot when dropped in water; chlorine is a thick, green gas.

◀ One of the most remarkable molecules is this molecule built from carbon atoms called a buckyball. It was constructed by scientists as an experiment but may well have practical uses in the future.

FACTS: About chemical bonds

Atomic nucleus

Electrons in their shells

Shared electrons

Sodium atom gives up an electron

Mutual electric attraction

Chlorine atom gains an electron

▲ Atoms are stable only when they have a full set of eight electrons in their outer shells. Atoms which have too many or too few can get a full set by sharing electrons with other atoms. This makes a covalent bond.

- **Valency**
  Each atom joins only with a certain number of others — as if each has only so many hooks it can hang others on. This number is called its 'valency'.

- **Chemical bonds**
  There are two main ways elements can combine: by sharing electrons in what are called 'covalent bonds', or by losing or gaining them in 'ionic bonds'. 'Metallic bonds' occur between huge numbers of atoms in a giant metallic lattice.

- **Ionic bonds**
  Ionic bonds occur when atoms with just a few electrons in their outer shells (page 202) donate them

▲ In ionic bonds, one atom donates an electron to another and so becomes negatively charged. The atoms are then bonded by mutual electrical attraction. This is what joins sodium atoms to chlorine atoms in salt.

to atoms with just a few missing from theirs. This makes the atom losing electrons positively charged and the other negatively charged — so they stick together by electrical attraction.

- **Covalent bonds**
  In covalent bonds, atoms share electrons. In water, two hydrogen atoms share electrons with one oxygen.

▲ *Some substances make acids when they dissolve in water. Weak acids, like lemon juice or vinegar, taste tart. Strong ones, like sulphuric acids are highly corrosive, burning, stinging and even dissolving metals. The opposites of acids are bases, known as alkalis when dissolved in water. Weak bases like baking powder taste bitter and feel soapy. Strong ones, like caustic soda, are as corrosive as acids. Chemists use 'indicators' such as litmus paper to test for acidity. Acids turn the paper red. Alkalis turn it blue.*

▼ *Strong acids are dangerous, but they can be useful in many ways. Sulphuric acid is used to make everything from fertilizers to paints. Crystals of salicylic acid (below), which occur naturally in willow trees, are used to make aspirin.*

FACTS: About water

▶ *Water molecules are made from two hydrogen atoms and an oxygen atom arranged in a V-shape. This is why the chemical formula is H_2O.*

- **Water poles**
  Water molecules are special. In sharing electrons with an oxygen atom, the electrons on each hydrogen atom are tugged to the side nearest the oxygen — leaving the far side 'bare', and exposing the positively charged nucleus. This gives water molecules a + (positive) and a - (negative) end, and so they are called polar molecules.

- **Hydrogen bonds**
  Pairs of water molecules bind together as + ends are drawn to - ends. These 'hydrogen' bonds keep water liquid to 100°C, at which heat most similar substances are gases.

The sequence of chemicals that make DNA's are coded instructions

▲ *The element carbon forms thousands of different compounds. Indeed, most of the 'organic' compounds on which life depends are carbon compounds. The most remarkable of these is deoxyribonucleic acid or DNA. DNA forms long molecules shaped like a twisted rope ladder. In the pattern of its rungs, DNA carries complete coded instructions for life — for everything from how a plant is to grow, to what colour your eyes should be.*

Key facts: Science

Milestones

- 300 BC: Greek mathematician Euclid lays down the principles of geometry still used today.
- 250 BC: Archimedes lays down the basic principles of physics.
- 1665–86: Isaac Newton introduces his theory of gravity and his three laws of motion.
- 1683: Anton van Leeuwenhoek discovers bacteria.
- 1789: Antoine Lavoisier makes the first list of chemical elements.
- 1804: Richard Trevithick builds the first steam loco.
- 1808: John Dalton proposes the atomic theory of matter.
- 1820: Hans Oersted finds that electricity creates a magnetic field.
- 1830: Joseph Henry and Michael Faraday find how electricity can be generated by a magnetic field.
- 1858: Charles Darwin suggests the theory of the evolution of species by natural selection.
- 1860s: Étienne Lenoir builds the first petrol engine car.
- 1865: James Clerk Maxwell suggests the idea of electromagnetic fields.
- 1869: Dmitri Mendeléev creates the Periodic Table of the elements.
- 1897: JJ Thomson discovers the electron.
- 1900: Max Planck invents quantum theory.
- 1903: Orville and Wilbur Wright make the first powered human aircraft flight.
- 1905: Albert Einstein invents the theory of relativity.
- 1911: Ernest Rutherford discovers the atomic nucleus.
- 1945: The first atomic bomb.
- 1953: Francis Crick and James Watson find the structure of the DNA molecule in every living cell.

Conversions

Conversion factors
To convert, multiply by the number shown

Length
- in to cm   2.54
- ft to m   0.3048
- yd to m   0.9144
- miles to km   1.6093
- cm to in   0.3937
- m to ft   3.2808
- m to yd   1.0936
- km to miles   0.6214

Weight
- oz to g   28.3495
- lb to kg   0.4536
- stones to kg   6.3503
- cwt to kg   50.802
- tons to tonnes   1.0161
- g to oz   0.0352
- kg to lb   2.2046
- kg to stones   0.1575
- kg to cwt   0.0197
- tonnes to tons   0.9842

Volume
- in^3 to cm^3 (cc)   16.3871
- ft^3 to litres   28.3169
- yd^3 to m^3 0.7646
- fl oz to m^3 28.4131
- pints to litres   0.5683
- gallons to litres   4.5461
- cm^3 to in^3 0.0610
- litres to ft^3 0.0353
- litres to pints   1.7598
- litres to gallons   0.2200

Fast, slow

Fast phenomonena

- Light — 299,792,458km per second
- Lightning — up to 50,400km per second
- Earth's orbit — 107,210 kmh
- Speed of sound in water — 1,440m per second
- Speed of sound in air — 342m per second at 18°C
- Skydiver — 1,000 kmh
- Jet stream — up to 700 kmh
- Tornado — 450 kmh
- Surface wind — 371 kmh

Fast machines

- Fastest steam locomotive — 202.8 kmh by the *Mallard* in 1934.
- Fastest train — 515.3 kmh by French TGV in 1990.
- Fastest road car — 349.21 kmh by Jaguar XJ220 in 1992.
- Fastest speed on land — 1,227.99 kmh by *Thrust SSC* in 1997.
- Fastest jet plane — 3,608 kmh by Lockheed SR-71A in 1990.
- Fastest airliner — 2,587 kmh by Russian Tupolev Tu-144.
- Fastest human flight — 39,897 kmh by crew of *Apollo 10* spacecraft in 1969.

Dead slow

- Fingernails grow at around 0.05cm a week.
- Toenails grow at about 0.01cm a week.
- Continents move at around 40cm a year.
- Snails move at up to 0.008 kmh.
- A tortoise moves at 0.27 kmh.
- Glaciers flow at 0.0005 kmh.
- Lichen grows at 0.0000000001 kmh.

Loud, soft

Loud noises

- Supernova explosion — 210 decibels
- Rocket launch — 180 db
- Toy guns — 170 db
- Jet taking off at 30m — 140 db
- Rock concert — 130 db
- Loud scream — 128 db
- Racing car — 125 db
- Dance club — 117 db
- Car horn — 110 db
- Chainsaw — 100 db
- Thunder — 90 db

Quiet sounds

- Ant breathing — less than 0 db
- The quietest we can hear — 0 db
- Rustling leaves — 10 db
- Quiet whisper — 12 db
- Average whisper — 20 db
- Conversation — 40 db
- Empty theatre — 45 db

Key facts: Science

Number power

Large and small numbers

•   Large numbers can have a huge number of digits. There are 17,000,000,000,000,000,000 water molecules in a single drop of water. So scientists often express large numbers in terms of 'powers' of 10. This is the number of times you have to multiply 10 by 10 to give the number. So 100 is 10 to the power to 2, which is written 10^2. 1,000 is 10 to the power 3, written 10^3, and so on.

• Tiny fractions can be written in the same way — as the number of times you have to divide 10 by 10 to give the fraction. So a hundredth is 10^{-2}. A thousandth is 10^{-3}, and so on.

Millions

• 1 million is 10 to the power 6 or 10^6.
• 10 million is 10 to the power 7 or 10^7.
• 7 million or 7×10^6 people live in London.
• The Sun is 1.5 million km or 1.5×10^6 km away.
• There are just over 31 million or 3.1×10^7 seconds in a year.

Billions

• 1 billion is 10 to the power 12 or 10^{12}.

• There are 6 billion or 6×10^{12} people in the world.
• There are 100 billion or 1×10^{14} brain cells in your brain.

Trillions

• 1 trillion is 10 to the power 15 or 10^{15}.
• Your body contains 25 trillion or 2.5×10^{16} red blood cells .
• A swarm of 12.5 trillion or 1.25×10^{16} locusts invaded Nebraska in 1875.

Quadrillions

• 1 quadrillion is 10 to the power 24 or 10^{24}.
• There are about 1 quadrillion or 10^{24} ants in the world.
• There are about 10 million quadrillion or 10^{30} molecules in a single apple.

Add-ons

These prefixes have number meanings, eg *kilo*watt and *mega*byte.

mega	10^6	
giga	10^9	
tera	10^{12}	
peta	10^{15}	
deca	10^1	exa	10^{18}
hecto	10^2	zetta	10^{21}
kilo	10^3	yotta	10^{24}

deca	10^1	exa	10^{18}
hecto	10^2	zetta	10^{21}
kilo	10^3	yotta	10^{24}

These prefixes mean different fractions, eg *milli*litre and *centi*metre.

micro	10^{-6}	
nano	10^{-9}	
pico	10^{-12}	
femto	10^{-15}	

deci	10^{-1}	atto	10^{-18}
centi	10^{-2}	zepto	10^{-21}
milli	10^{-3}	yocto	10^{-24}

Cold, hot

Cold and hot points	°C	°F	K
Coldest possible temperature (atoms stop moving)	–273.15	–459.67	0
Coldest temperature achieved in a laboratory	–272.999	–459.399	2
Helium melts	–272.2	–458	3
Outer space	–270	–457	4
Helium boils	–268.9	–452	5
Nitrogen melts	–209.86	–344	67
Coldest weather recorded on Earth	–89.2	–128.6	183.8
Water freezes	0	32	273.15
Butter melts	30	90	300
Human body temperature	37	98.6	310
Hottest weather recorded on Earth	58	136.4	331
Water boils	100	212	373.15
Surface of Venus	480	890	750
Coal fire burns	800	1,500	1,100
Iron melts	1,535	2,795	1,808
Gas flame burns	1,600	3,000	1,900
Molten lava	1,700	3,200	2,000
Carbon melts	3,550	6,422	3820
Surface of the Sun	6,000	10,000	6,000
Centre of the Earth	16,000	30,000	16,000
Lightning	30,000	54,000	30,000
Centre of a star	100 mill	180 mill	100 mill
Centre of an H-bomb	400 mill	700 mill	400 mill

Tiny, big

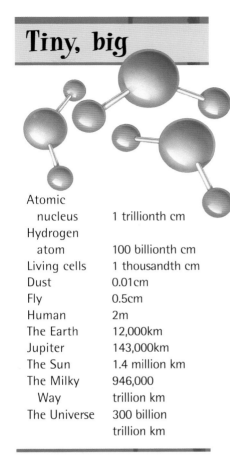

Atomic nucleus	1 trillionth cm
Hydrogen atom	100 billionth cm
Living cells	1 thousandth cm
Dust	0.01cm
Fly	0.5cm
Human	2m
The Earth	12,000km
Jupiter	143,000km
The Sun	1.4 million km
The Milky Way	946,000 trillion km
The Universe	300 billion trillion km

Light, heavy

Photon	5.3×10^{-63} kg
Oxygen atom	3×10^{-26} kg
Ant	10^{-5} kg
Human	10^2 kg
Elephant	10^4 kg
Blue whale	10^5 kg
Oil tanker	10^8 kg
The Earth	6×10^{24} kg
The Sun	2×10^{30} kg
The Galaxy	2×10^{41} kg
The Universe	10^{51} kg

Quiz: Science

1. What is the boiling point of water?

2. Lightning is the release of a huge charge of what kind of electricity?

3. Who made the first magnetic compasses and used them for fortune telling and direction finding?

4. Iron loses its magnetism above 760°C: true or false?

5. Every magnet has two poles, no matter what its shape: true or false?

6. The Earth's magnetic North Pole is a long way from the North Pole: true or false?

7. What do solar cells do?

8. Uranium is a radioactive material. Does it occur naturally or is it artificially made?

9. When light rays are bent by something like glass or water, what is this called?

10. The angle that light strikes a mirror is called the angle of incidence: true or false?

11. What is the name of the force that holds you on the ground?

12. How many Laws of Motion did Isaac Newton find?

13. What does HEP stand for?

14. Does heat make things contract or expand?

15. Scientists think quarks are stuck together by gluons: true or false?

16. All particles are either quarks or leptons: true or false?

17. Chemists can try out new molecules on computer screens: true or false?

18. On the Kelvin scale used by scientists, water freezes at 273.15 K: true or false?

19. What is the name given to the Southern Lights (the aurora) over the South Pole?

20. What is produced when two or more elements join together?

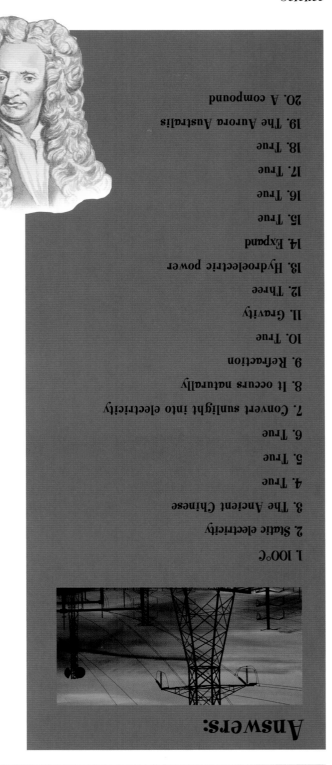

Answers:

1. 100°C
2. Static electricity
3. The Ancient Chinese
4. True
5. True
6. True
7. Convert sunlight into electricity
8. It occurs naturally
9. Refraction
10. True
11. Gravity
12. Three
13. Hydroelectric power
14. Expand
15. True
16. True
17. True
18. True
19. The Aurora Australis
20. A compound

INDEX

exosphere 151
extensor 16, 17
eye 20
Eyre, Lake 175

F

Fahrenheit 199
fairy fly 71
Fallopian tube 24
Fallopio, Gabriel 39
false fruits 84
false morel 97
fangs 66
Faraday, Michael 208
farm animals 60-61
fast twitch red muscle 17
fats 29
faults 169
feet, footprints 40
feldspar 162
femur 19, 38
ferns 94-95, 106, 107
fertilizers 99
fever 31
feverfew 103
fibula 19
fig 108
filament 183
Finland 175
firs 92
fish 59, 74
fission 188
flare 119
Fleming, Alexander 40
flexor 16, 17
flight 208, 209
floodplain 170
Florey, Howard 40
flour 100, 101
flowers 84-87, 106, 108, 197
fluorine 163
fly agaric 97
flying frog 68
foetus 25
fold mountains 168
food 26-29, 100-101,

108
force 194-195
forests 73
formic acid 70
formula (chemical) 205
fossil fuels 108, 161, 197
fossils 121, 158
fowl 61
fox 54
foxglove 103
fractions 210
France 175
freezing point 211
frill-necked lizard 67
frog 68, 69
fronds 94, 95
fronts (weather) 152
fruit and vegetables 29, 100
fruits 84-85, 89
fulcrum 193
fungi 31, 34, 72, 81, 91, 96-97, 98, 107
fur 46
fusion 188

G

Gaboon viper 66
Gagarin, Yuri 137
Galapagos 67
galaxies 8, 9, 130-131, 133, 134, 135, 138, 139
Galilean moons 122
Galileo 122, 140
Galileo space probe 137
Galle, John 125, 140
gamma rays 188
garden flowers 86
garlic 103
gases 200-201
gastric juices 27
Gavarnie Falls 174
gears 192
gecko 67
gems 162
General Sherman 89, 108

generators 182
genetic engineering 35
gentoo penguin 74
geodes 162
geoid 114
geological column 158
geologists 158
geometry 208
geostationary orbit 137
Germany 174, 175
germs 30, 31, 34, 35
geysers 165
giant salamander 69, 75
giant stars 128, 132
gibbon 53
ginger 103
gingko 92
giraffe 75
glaciers 169, 177
glades 91
glass 190
Glass Falls 174
gluons 212
gluteus maximus 16, 38
GNP 175
goat 60
Goddard, Robert 143
gold 163, 205, 206
goldfish 59
Goliath beetle 75
Goliath frog 68
goose 61, 64
gorilla 53
gorse 86
grains 160, 162
Grand Canyon 170
granite 160, 162
granules 119
grapes 84
graphite 183
grass 82
grasslands 73, 109
gravity 117, 124, 131, 132, 133, 136, 137, 138, 139, 172, 194, 195, 202
grazing animals 49
Great Barrier Reef 9

Great Bear 129
Great Bear Lake 175
Great Britain 176
Great Falls 174
Great Red Spot 122
Great Slave Lake 175
Great Wall 8
Greece, ancient 103
greenhouse effect 121
Greenland 176
Greenwich, England 148
grizzly bear 55
groundsel 87
Groups (galaxies) 131
groyne 172
guinea pig 47
Guinea-Bissau 175
Gulf of Mexico 177
guppies 59
gut see alimentary canal
guyots 173
gymnosperms 92, 107
gyromitrin 97

H

haemoglobin 12
half-life 189
Halley's comet 127
hammer see malleus
hamster 59
Hanuman langur 52
hardwood 89
harrier 65
Harvey, William 39
hay fever 31
headlands 172
hearing 21
heart 12-13, 17, 37, 39
heart attack 13
heart transplant 36, 40
heart-lung machine 40
heartwood 88
heat 198-199, 200, 211
height 38
helium 122, 124, 211
hemispheres 149

Local Group 131
Logan 175
London 174
longitude 148
lunar eclipse 115
lungs 14-15, 17, 39
Luxembourg 175
lymph 30
lymphatic system 30
lymphocytes 12, 30

M

macaw 63
machines 192-193
macrophages 31
Madagascar 52, 176
Magellanic Clouds 131
magenta 191
magma 161, 164, 165
magma chamber 164
magnetic dip 184
magnetic field 118, 122, 184, 208
Magnetic North 184
magnetism 182, 184, 185, 188
magnetosphere 184
magnetron 189
magnets 182, 184-185
Mai-Ndombe, Lake 175
maidenhair tree 89, 92
Main Sequence stars 128
maize 100, 101
Malawi 175
malleus 21
Malphigi, Marcello 39
mammals 46-49, 56-57, 75
manatee 57
manganese 162
mantle, Earth's 115, 156
Maracaibo, Lake 175
Marattia 95
marble 160
Mardalsfossen 174
margay 51
Margherita Peak 175

Marianas trench 173
marrow 19
Mars 120, 121, 136, 137, 140, 143
Mars Pathfinder 136, 137
mass 195
matriarch 48
matter 133, 138, 139, 195, 200, 202-203, 208
Matterhorn 9, 169
Maxwell, James Clerk 208
Mayer, Michael 140
meadows 86
meanders 170, 171
measles 35
measurements 8
mechanical advantage 192, 193
medicine 102, 103
Mediterranean 172, 177
medulla 22
megabytes 210
megaphyllous leaves 95
Meissner's corpuscles 21
melting point 200
memory 22
Mendeléev, Dmitri 208
menstruation 24
Mercalli scale 167
Mercury 120, 140
meridians 148
Merino 61
Merkel's discs 21
merychippus 159
mesosphere 151, 156
Mesozoic Era 159
mesquite 104
Messina, Italy 166
metallic bonds 206
metals 205, 207
metamorphic rock 160, 161
metamorphosis 69
meteor shower 126
meteorites 126-127
meteors 120, 123, 126

methane 124
Mexico 174
Mexico City 174
mica 162
Michigan, Lake 175
microchips 187
microprocessors 186
microsurgery 37
microwaves 188, 189
mid-ocean spreading 157
mildew 96
milk 46, 61
Milky Way 9, 130, 131
millet 100
minerals 29, 162-163
mint 103
mirror 190
Mississippi-Missouri River 171
mistletoe 82
Mohorovicic discontinuity 156
molecules 198, 199, 200, 201, 203, 206, 207
Moluccas 103
momentum 194
Monerans 72
monkeys 52-3
Monocotyledons 106
monotremes 46
month, lunar 116
Moon 116-117, 119, 134, 135, 172
Moon landings 117, 137
moons 122, 123, 124, 132, 142
morphine 103
Moscow 174
mosses 94-95, 107
moth 70
motion 194-195
moulds 34, 72, 96
mountains 9, 73, 109, 168-169, 175
mouse 47
mouse (computer) 187
mouth 27
movement 22

Mozambique 175
MRI scans 33
Mt Cook 175
Mt Everest 169, 175
Mt Kilimanjaro 169, 175
Mt McKinley 169, 175
Mt St Helens 165
Mt Tamboro 165
Mt Toba 165
Mt Vesuvius 165
Mt Wilhelm 169
multiple births 38
muscarine 97
muscles 15, 16-17, 27, 38
mushrooms 96-97
mute swan 74
Mycetae 96
myofibril 16, 17
myosin 16, 17

N

nappe 168
NASA 121
natural gas 171, 197
natural selection 208
nebulae 130, 131
neck 40
nectar 70, 71
needles 92
Nepal 175
Neptune 124-125, 137, 140
nerves 22, 23
nervous system 23
neurons 23
neurotransmitters 23
neutron stars 128
neutrons 188, 202
neutrophils 12, 30
New Guinea 176
New World monkeys 52
New York 174
newt 69
Newton, Isaac 195, 208
Nicaragua, Lake 175
nickel 156, 184

Nigeria 174
Nile river 171
nitrogen 41, 124, 204, 211
nitrous oxide 197
noble gases 204, 205
noise 209
North America 174
North Pole 148, 184, 185
North Sea 177
northern lights see Aurorea Borealis
Norway 175
nuclear energy 182, 188, 197
nuclear fission 188
nuclear fusion 188
nuclear reactions 118
nuclei 188, 202, 208
numbers 210
nutmeg 103
nuts 89
Nyasa, Lake 175

O

oak tree 89, 91
oats 101
oblate spheroid 114
Oceania 174
oceans 73, 172-173, 177
Oersted, Hans 208
oesophagus 27
oil 161, 197
Ojos del Salado 175
Old World monkeys 52
olfactory nerve 21
olives 100
olivine 163
Olympus Mons 121
Onega, Lake 175
onion 82, 83
Ontario, Lake 175
opaque 190
open universe idea 138
opium 103
opthalmoscope 32

optic nerve 20
orang-utan 53
oranges 100
orbit 120, 123, 125, 132, 137, 148
orchid 86
Ordovician Period 158
oregano 103
Orion 129, 130
osprey 65
ossicles 21
osteoblasts 19
osteoclasts 19
osteocytes 18
osteons 19
ostrich 74
ovaries (human) 24
ovaries (plant) 84, 89, 106
ovulation 25
ovules 84
ovum 24, 25
owl 65
oxygen 12, 14, 15, 17, 25, 41, 81, 163, 207

P

pacemakers 37
Pacific Ocean 172, 173, 177
paddy fields 101
Pakistan 174
palaeomagnetism 184
palm tree 90, 108
pancreas 27
panda 54, 55
parachutes 194
Paradise whydah 63
parallaxes 134, 135
parallels 148
parasites 82, 96
Paris 174
parrot 63
parsecs 134
particle accelerators 139
Patos 175
pea crab 74

pear 84
peat 95
Pegasus constellation 129
pelican 62
pelvis 18, 19
penguin 74
penicillin 34, 40
penis 24
peregrine falcon 65, 74
perennials 87
perihelian 149
Periodic Table 204, 208
Periodics (comets) 127
Periods (geological time) 158
Periods (P Table) 204
periosteum 19
peristalsis 27
periwinkle 103
Permian Period 159
PET scans 189
petal 85
Petermanns Glacier 177
petiole 80
petrol 197, 208
pets 58-59
phalanges 19
phalloidine 97
pharynx 14
phases 117
pheasant 64
Philippines 174
phloem 80
phosphate 19
phosphor 186
photons 191
photosphere 118
photosynthesis 81, 197
phylloplankton 99
physics 208
physiology 39
phytoplankton 99
Piazzi, Giuseppi 140
pig 46, 60
pigeon 65
pine trees 92, 93
Pioneer II 137
piranha 59
pistil 106

placenta 25
Planck, Max 208
planets 120-125, 129, 134, 135, 139, 140
plankton 99
plant environments 109
plant kingdom 107
Plantae 72
plantations 92
plants 48, 80-109, 197
plasma 12, 39
plastron 67
platelets 12, 39
Plough (constellation) 129
plover 64
plum 84
Pluto 124, 125, 134, 140
plutonium 189
pods 84
poison-arrow frog 68
polar bear 55
polar molecules 207
Pole Star 129
poles 114, 148, 184, 185
poles (magnetic) 184
polio 35, 40
pollen 71, 84, 85, 89, 93, 106
pollination 85, 87, 105
Pompeii 165
pons 22
poppy 85, 103
population 174
porcupine 47
porphyra 99
porpoise 56
potato 82, 83, 100
poultry 61
power stations 182
Precambrian era 158, 159
pregnancy 25
prehensile tail 52
pressure 21, 199, 200
prickly pear 104
primary colours 191

Acknowledgements

All photographs from
Miles Kelly Archive